D0469038

Naguib Mahfouz

TRANSLATED BY

Denys Johnson-Davies

⚓ Anchor Books   DOUBLEDAY

New York   London   Toronto   Sydney   Auckland

Echoes

OF AN *Autobiography*

AN ANCHOR BOOK
PUBLISHED BY DOUBLEDAY
a division of Bantam Doubleday Dell Publishing Group, Inc.
1540 Broadway, New York, New York 10036

ANCHOR BOOKS, DOUBLEDAY, *and the portrayal of an anchor*
are trademarks of Doubleday,
a division of Bantam Doubleday Dell
Publishing Group, Inc.

BOOK DESIGN BY TERRY KARYDES

Title page photo:
Cairo, Egypt: Doorway of a Citadel. An undated photo.
Credit: Corbis-Bettmann.

Echoes of an Autobiography *was originally published by Doubleday in 1997.*
The Anchor Books edition is published by arrangement with Doubleday.

The Library of Congress has cataloged the hardcover edition of this book as follows:
Mahfūz, Najīb, 1912–
Echoes of an autobiography / Naguib Mahfouz;
translated by Denys Johnson-Davies.
p.   cm.
"First serialized in Arabic in al-Ahram in 1994
as Aṣdā' al-sīrah al-dhātiyah"—CIP t.p. verso.
1. Mahfūz, Najīb, 1912–   —Biography.
2. Authors, Arab—Egypt—Biography.
I. Johnson-Davies, Denys.   II. Title.
PJ7846.A46Z463   1997   892'.736—dc20
[B]   96-12386   CIP

ISBN 0-385-48556-5
Copyright © 1994 by Naguib Mahfouz
English translation copyright © 1997 by the American University in Cairo Press
Foreword copyright © 1997 by Nadine Gordimer

First published in Egypt in 1997 by
The American University in Cairo Press
113 Sharia Kasr el-Aini, Cairo, Egypt

First serialized in Arabic in al-Ahram *in 1994 as* Asdaa' al-sira al-dhatiyya
Protected under the Berne Convention

The Dialogue of Late Afternoon

NADINE GORDIMER

I have visited Egypt three times in my life and have never met Naguib Mahfouz. The first times, 1954 and 1958, I had not heard of him or his work; by the third time, 1993, all his work available in English translation was deeply familiar to me and counted, in my canon, as part of the few great international contemporary literary achievements. In 1993 I had asked my kind hosts to arrange for us to meet, but in their zeal to make me welcome they planned for this to happen at a large gathering with other Egyptian writers, and

Naguib Mahfouz, by temperament and in the deserved privacy of old age, does not attend such public events. My days in Cairo were few and there was not time to seek another opportunity. It does not matter. The essence of a writer's being is in the work, not the personality, though the world values things otherwise, and would rather see what the writer looks like on television than read where he or she really is to be found: in the writings.

I am inclined to believe that a similar valuation may be applied to autobiography. The writer's gift to fellow humans is his or her gifts, the bounty of the creative imagination which comes from no one knows where or why. The persona of the writer is the vessel. Whether it is flamboyantly decorated by a lifestyle of excess in alcoholism, adventurism, sexual experiment, or whether it is sparsely chased by what appears to be domestic dullness, its content has been poured into the work; the truth of it is there. (Sometimes in spite of the author . . .) Of course there are exceptions, but in general fiction writers who produce autobiographies are those whose autobiographies are better than their novels. Which has something to indicate about the limitation of their gifts. Let the *biographers* trace the chronology of life from the circumstances of the birth to the honoured or forgotten grave. What that span produced is already extant, transformed, freed from place and time.

The aphorisms, parables, allegories in this work of Naguib Mahfouz have no dates appended. It's of no account when he wrote them. The back-and-forth of a mind creating its consciousness expands and contracts, rather than roves between past and present, with a totality which is not merely memory. Indeed, with the wry humour that flashes through profundity in all his thinking, Mahfouz meets memory as "an enormous person with a stomach as large as the ocean, and a mouth that could swallow an elephant. I asked him in amazement, 'Who are you, sir?' He answered with surprise, 'I am forgetfulness. How could you have forgotten me?' " The *totality* is the comprehension of past and present experience as elements which exist contemporaneously. These pieces are meditations which echo that which was, has been, and is the writer, Mahfouz. They are—in the words of the title of one of the prose pieces—"The Dialogue of Late Afternoon" of his life. I don't believe any autobiography, with its inevitable implication of self-presentation, could have matched what we have here.

If the prose pieces have no dates they do each have a title, and these in themselves are what one might call the *essence of the essence* of Mahfouz's discoveries in and contemplation of life. The preoccupations so marvelously explored in his fiction appear almost ideographically (if this is not an unacceptable oxymoron!), the single word or phrase standing for morality, justice, time, religion, memory, sensuality, beauty, ambition, death, freedom. And all these are regarded through a changing focus: narrowing briefly to the cynical; taking the middle distance of humour and affection; opening wide to reverence. Prompted by his own words—another title, "The Train of the Unexpected"—I take the liberty of paraphrasing myself in what I have remarked[1] elsewhere of Mahfouz: he has the gift of only great writers to

---

[1] "Zaabalawi: The Concealed Side," from *Writing and Being,* Nadine Gordimer. Harvard University Press, 1995.

contemplate all the possibilities inherent in life rather than discard this or that awkwardness for consistency. The stimulus of his writing comes from the conflict of responses he elicits.

In "A Man Reserves a Seat" a bus from a working-class suburb and a private car from a wealthy one set out for Cairo's station at the same moment, and arrive at the same time, colliding in an accident in which both are slightly damaged. But a man passing between the two is crushed and dies. "He was crossing the square in order to book a seat on the train going to Upper Egypt." As one reads this laconic concluding sentence, almost an aside, the title suddenly leaps out, heavy type, in all the complexity of the many meanings it may carry. I read it thus: rich and poor arrive at the same point in human destiny whatever their means. Even the man who travels with neither, seeking to pass between the two, cannot escape; you cannot reserve a seat in destiny. There is no escape from the human condition; the final destination of which is death.

Naguib Mahfouz is an old man and it would be natural for him to reflect on that destiny/destination, inescapable for believers and unbelievers alike. But those of us who know his work know that he always has had death in mind as part of what life itself is. We are all formed by the social structures which are the corridors through which we are shunted, and it is a reflection of the power of bureaucracy, the Egyptian civil service as regulator of existence and the height of ambition for a prestigious career, that his allegory of death should be entitled "The Next Posting." The question with which the allegory ends is one he may be asking himself now, but that he has contemplated for his fictional characters much earlier: "Why did you not prepare yourself for it when you knew it was your inevitable destiny?" It is said—perhaps *he* has said, although he takes care to evade interviews and "explanations" of his work—that Marcel Proust has influenced him. "Shortly Before Dawn," "Happiness" and "Music" are disparate encounters in old age, where we shall not be recognizable to one another, as in the final gathering at the end of *A la Recherche du Temps Perdu,* but the mood is unproustian in the compensation that something vivid remains from what one has lost. In "Music" the singer has been forgotten but the *tawashih* music she sang is still a delight. Life takes up the eternal, discards the temporal.

Politics: almost as inevitable as death, in account of a lifetime in Mahfouz's span and ours, children of the twentieth century. The morality of politics is intricately and inextricably knotted to the morality of personal relations in Mahfouz's masterpiece, *The Cairo Trilogy,* and in some of his lesser works. Here, in "Layla" (the title is the woman's name) sexual morality is another strand. "In the days of the struggle of ideas" Layla was a controversial woman. "An aura of beauty and allurement" surrounded her, and while some saw her as a liberated pioneer, others criticised her as nothing but an immoral woman. "When the sun set and the struggle and the ideas disappeared from sight . . . many emigrated . . . Years later they returned, each armed with a purse of gold and a cargo of disrepute." Layla laughs, and enquires, "I wonder what you have to say now about immorality?" The essential question, "When will the state of the country be sound?" is answered: "When its people believe that the end result of cowardice is more disastrous than that of behaving with integrity." But this politico-moral imperative is not so easy to follow. In a political dispute ("The Challenge") a minister in government is asked, "Can you show me a person who is clean and unsullied?," and the answer comes: "You need but one example of many—children, the idiotic, and the mad—and the world's still doing fine."

Again, Mahfouz's surprise about-face startles, flipping from biting condemnation to—what? Irony, cynicism, accusatory jeers at ourselves? Or is there a defiance there? The defiance of survival, if not "doing fine" morally, then as expressed by the courtesan in "Question and Answer" who says, "I used to sell love at a handsome profit, and I came to buy it at considerable loss. I have no other choice with this wicked but fascinating life." In "Eternity" one of the beggars, outcast sheikhs and blind men who wander through Mahfouz's works as the elusive answer to salvation, says "With the setting of each sun I lament my wasted days, my declining countries, and my transitory gods." It is a cry of mourning for the world that Mahfouz sounds here; but not an epitaph, for set against it is the perpetuation, no choice, of "this wicked but fascinating life."

At a seminar following a lecture I gave on Mahfouz's *Cairo Trilogy* at Harvard a few years ago, some feminists attacked his depiction of women characters in the novels; they were outraged at the spectacle of Amina, Al-Sayid Ahmad Abd al-Jawad's wife, forbidden to leave the family house unless in the company of her husband, and at the account of the fate of the girls in the family, married off to men of Abd al-Jawad's choice without any concern for their own feelings, and without the possibility of an alternative independent existence. The students were ready to deny the genius of the novel on these grounds. It was a case of killing the messenger: Mahfouz was relaying the oppression of Amina and her daughters as it existed; he was not its advocate. His

insight to the complex socio-sexual mores, the seraglio-
prison that distorted the lives of women members of Abd al-
Jawad's family was a protest far more powerful than that of
those who accused him of literary chauvinism.

In this present garnering of the values of Mahfouz's lifetime, woman is the symbol not only of beauty and joy in
being alive but also of spiritual release. This is personified
as—in celebration, not male patronage—"a naked woman
with the bloom of the nectar of life" who has "the heart of
music as her site." The Proustian conception (let us grant
it, even if only coincidence with Mahfouz's own) of love as
pain/joy, inseparably so, has a Mahfouzian wider reference
as a part of the betrayal by time itself, let alone any lover.
Entitled "Mercy," the aperçu reflects on an old couple:
"They were brought together by love thirty years ago, then it
had abandoned them along with the rest of their expectations."

Love of the world, "this wicked but fascinating life," is
the dynamism shown to justify itself as essential to religious
precepts sometimes in its very opposition to them. The
greed for life is admissible to Mahfouz in all his work;
against which, of course, there is juxtaposed *excess as unfulfil-
ment*. Yet how unashamedly joyous is the parable of "The
Bridegroom": "I asked Sheik Abd-Rabbih al-Ta'ih about
his ideal among those people with whom he had been closely
associated, and he said: 'A good man whose miracles were
manifested by his perseverance in the service of people and
the remembrance of God; on his hundredth birthday he
drank, danced, sang, and married a virgin of twenty. And on
the wedding night there came a troop of angels who perfumed him with incense from the mountains of Qaf at the
end of the earth.' "

It is detachment that sins against life. When the narrator tells the Sheikh "I heard some people holding against you your intense love for the world," the Sheikh answers "Love of the world is one of the signs of gratitude, and evidence of a craving for everything beautiful." Yet this is no rosy denial that life is sad: "It has been decreed that man shall walk staggeringly between pleasure and pain." Decreed by whom? Is the responsibility for this perhaps aleatory, cosmic rather than religious, if one may make such a distinction? And there is the question of mortality, since nowhere in these stoic but not materialist writings is there expressed any belief in after-life, or any desire for it; paradise is not an end for which earthly existence is the means. This life, when explored and embraced completely and fearlessly by tender sceptic and obdurate pursuer of salvation Naguib Mahfouz, is enough. Mortality becomes the Sheikh's serene and exquisite image: "There is nothing between the lifting of the veil from the face of the bride and the lowering of it over her corpse but a moment that is like a heartbeat." And after a premonition of death one night, all the Sheikh asks of God, instead of eternal life, is "well-being, out of pity for people who were awaiting my help the following day."

If sensuality in the wider sense of all its forms is not an element opposed to, apart from, spirituality, there is at the same time division *within that acceptance,* for life itself is conceived by Mahfouz as a creative tension between desires and moral precepts. On the one hand, sensuality is the spirit of life, life-force; on the other abstinence is the required condition to attain spirituality.

It is said that Mahfouz has been influenced by Sufism. My own acquaintance with Sufism is extremely superficial, confined to an understanding that its central belief is that the awakening to the inner life of man is a necessary condition of fulfilment as a human being, while the outer and inner realities are inseparable. Readers like myself may receive Sufism through the transmission of Mahfouz as, for precedent, anyone who is not a Christian may receive Christian beliefs in the *Pensées:* through Pascal. (And by the way, there is a direct connection there, between the paths of the Sufi and the Christian. Pascal: "To obtain anything from God, the external must be joined to the internal.") Faith, no matter what its doctrine, takes on the contours of individual circumstance, experience, and the meditation upon these of the adherent. We therefore may take manifestations of Sufi religious philosophy that are to be discerned in Mahfouz's thinking as more likely to be his own gnosis, original rather than doctrinal. There is surely no heresy in this; only celebration of the doubled creativity: a resplendent intelligence applied to the tenets of what has to be taken on faith.

If we are to take a definitive reading of where Mahfouz stands in relation to faith, I think we must remember what his most brilliantly conceived character, Kamal, has declared in *The Cairo Trilogy:* "The choice of a faith still has not been decided. The great consolation I have is that it is not over yet." For Mahfouz life is a search in which one must find one's own sign-posts. The text for this is his story "Zaabalawi."[2] When a sick man goes on a pilgrimage

---

[2] "Zaabalawi," from *The Time and the Place, and other stories*, Naguib Mahfouz. Doubleday, 1991.

through ancient Cairo to seek healing from the saintly Sheikh Zaabalawi, everybody he asks for directions sends him somewhere different. Told at last he will find the saint (who is also dissolute: see unity-in-dichotomy, again) in a bar, the weary man falls asleep waiting for him to appear. When he wakes, he finds his head wet. The drinkers tell him Zaabalawi came while he was asleep and sprinkled water on him to refresh him. Having had this sign of Zaabalawi's existence, the man will go on searching for him all his life— "Yes, I have to find Zaabalawi."

The second half of the prose in the present collection is devoted to the utterances and experiences of another Sheikh, one Abd-Rabbih al-Ta'ih, who as his spokesman is perhaps Naguib Mahfouz's imagined companion of some of the saintly sages in Sufi history, such as Rabi'a al-Adawiya (a woman) of Basra, Imam Junayd al-Baghdadi of Persia, Khwaja Mu'in'ud-Din Chisti of India, Sheikh Muzaffer of Istanbul. He is also, surely, Zaabalawi, and brother of all the other wanderers who appear and disappear to tantalize the yearning for meaning and salvation in the streets of Mahfouz's works, offering and withdrawing fragments of answer to the mystery of existence, and guidance on how to live it well. This one, when first he makes his appearance in the quarter of Cairo invented for Mahfouz's notebooks, is heard to call out: "A stray one has been born, good fellows." The essence of this stray one's teaching is in his response to the narrator, Everyman, rather than Mahfouz, who gives as his claim to join the Sheikh's Platonic cave of followers, "I have all but wearied of the world and wish to flee from it." The Sheikh says, "Love of the world is the core of our brotherhood and our enemy is flight."

One of the Sheikh's adages is: "The nearest man comes to his Lord is when he is exercising his freedom correctly." Many of Mahfouz's parables are of the intransigence of authority and the hopelessness of merely petitioning the powers of oppression. With the devastating "After You Come Out of Prison" one can't avoid comparison with Kafka, although I have tried to do so since Kafka is invoked to inflate the false profundity of any piece of whining against trivial frustrations. In answer to a journalist's question, "What is the subject closest to your heart?" Mahfouz gave one of the rare responses in his own person: "Freedom. Freedom from colonization, freedom from the absolute rule of kings, basic human freedom in the context of society and family. These types of freedom follow one from the other." This love of freedom breathes from every line in this book. It is imbued with what his character Kamal has called "a struggle towards truth aiming at the good of mankind as a whole . . . life would be meaningless without that," and with the tolerance Kamal's friend Husayn has defined: "The believer derives his love for these values from religion, while the free man loves them for themselves."

Whatever your personal hermeneutics, it is impossible to read this work without gaining, with immense pleasure and in all gratitude, illumination through a quality that has come to be regarded as a quaint anachronism in modern existence, where information is believed to have taken its place. I pronounce with hesitation: wisdom. Mahfouz has it. It dangles before us a hold on the mystery. Mahfouz is himself a Zaabalawi.

Echoes

OF AN

Autobiography

A Prayer

I was less than seven years old when I said a prayer for the revolution.

One morning I went to my primary school, escorted by the maid. I walked like someone being led off to prison. In my hand was a copybook, in my eyes a look of dejection, in my heart a longing for anarchy. The cold air stung my half-naked legs below my shorts. We found the school closed, with the janitor saying in a stentorian voice, "Because of the demonstrations there will again be no school today."

A wave of joy flowed over me and swept me to the shores of happiness.

From the depths of my heart I prayed to God that the revolution might last forever.

A Lament

Death paid its first visit to our home when my grand-
mother died. Death was still something new: I had had
no experience of it except in passing on the street. I knew
the old adage that it was inevitable, that there was no escap-
ing it, but my real feelings saw it as being as remote as the
sky from the earth. Sobs wrested me from my state of calm as
I realized that it had slipped, unbeknown to us, into that
room that had recounted to me such beautiful stories.

I saw myself as small and death as a giant, its breath
coming and going in all the rooms, for every person re-
members it, every person tells of it.

I tired of the chase and took refuge in my room to savor
a minute of quiet and solitude. And then the door opened
and the beautiful girl with the long black braid entered and
whispered tenderly, "Don't stay on your own."

A sudden feeling of revolt flared up inside me; it was
marked by violence and it yearned for madness. I grasped
hold of her hand and drew it to my chest with all the sadness
and fear that surged within me.

An Old Debt

In my youth I succumbed to an illness that persisted for
several months. The atmosphere around me changed dra-
matically, as did the way people treated me. Gone was the
world of intimidation as I was taken into the embrace of

tender attention. My mother would not leave me on my own and my father would stop and see me as he came and went, while my brothers and sisters brought me presents. There was no scolding or reproach about failing examinations.

When I was on the way to recovery I was very afraid that I would go back to the former hell. Thereupon, a new individual was created within me, who was determined to preserve the atmosphere of tenderness and esteem. If application was the key to happiness, then let me apply myself, whatever the cost in hardship; thus I began to leap from one success to another, with everyone becoming my friends and loved ones.

How rare for an illness to score such beautiful achievements as mine.

The Next Posting

"I have come to you because you are my first and last refuge," he said urgently.

"This means that you come with a new request," said the old man, smiling.

"My transfer from the governorate has been decided upon as the next posting."

"Haven't you spent there the period as laid down by law? These are the conventions followed in your position."

"Being transferred would be harmful to me and my family," he entreated.

"I informed you of the nature of your work from the very first day."

"The fact is that the governorate has become like home to us, and we can't do without it."

"That is what your colleagues, past and yet to come, say, and you know that the time for your transfer cannot be put forward or back."

"What a cruel experience," he said in grief.

"Why did you not prepare yourself for it when you knew it was your inevitable destiny?"

The Crossroads

At our house I came to know the Bey's mother. Even today I don't know her real name, only that she was my aunt, the Bey's mother. She would sit in her room on a sofa, heavily veiled and fingering her prayer beads. Whenever I craved some additional pocket money I would slip along to where she sat.

From time to time a car would come to a stop in front of our small house and the Bey would get out: short, dignified, and solemn. He would kiss his mother's hand and receive her blessing. His visit would animate the house with a breath of joy and fun, and it might bring with it a box of sweets for me.

Another man would pay a regular visit to the Bey's mother every Friday. He was the spitting image of the Bey, but he would usually be dressed in a gallabiya, slippers with turned-up toes, and a skullcap, while his face had all the signs of someone down on his luck. My aunt would greet him formally and would seat him beside her in the place of honor.

I was confused by him.

My mother would warn me not to play in the room while he was there.

In the end she had to whisper to me, "He's your aunt's son."

"The Bey's brother?" I asked in consternation.

"Yes," she answered clearly, "and give him as much respect as you give to the Bey."

He came to arouse in me even more curiosity than the Bey himself.

The Good Old Times

We were all boys living in the same street, our ages ranging from eight to ten. He stood out because of a bodily strength that was beyond his years, and he would apply himself ardently to developing his muscles with weight lifting. He was a boorish, coarse, and quarrelsome boy, ready to pick a fight for the most trivial of reasons. No day passed peacefully without a battle and without him beating one of us up. Thus he became in our lives a specter of torment and trouble.

You can therefore well imagine our great joy when we learned that his family had decided to leave the quarter altogether. We truly felt that we were beginning a new life of affection, felicity, and peace. We continued to have news of him, however, for he took up sports professionally and excelled at them, winning several championships, until he was forced to retire because of a heart condition. We then almost forgot him, by reason of the vicissitudes of old age and the passage of time.

As I was sitting at a café in al-Husayn, I was surprised to see him approaching, bearing his long life and visible debility.

He saw me, recognized me, and smiled. Without being invited, he sat down. He appeared to be in an animated state as he began calculating the many years during which we had not seen one another. He went on asking about those relatives and friends he remembered. Then he sighed and asked nostalgically, "Do you remember the good old times we had?"

Forgetfulness

Who is this old man who leaves his home each morning to walk about, getting as much exercise as he can?

He is the sheikh, the teacher of Arabic, who was retired more than twenty years ago.

Whenever he feels tired he sits down on the pavement, or on the stone wall of the garden of a house, leaning on his stick and drying his sweat with the end of his flowing gallabiya. The quarter knows him and the people love him; but seldom does anyone greet him, because of his weak memory and senses. He has forgotten relatives and neighbors, students and the rules of grammar.

The Singer

My heart is with the handsome young singer. Standing in the middle of the lane, he would begin singing in a melodious voice:

The pretty one is coming.

Quickly the blurred shapes of women would appear behind the chinks in the windows, while men's eyes would emit sparks of disapproval.

The young man would continue on happily, followed by exclamations of love and death.

Shortly Before Dawn

The two of them would sit cross-legged on the same sofa. They would chat in cheerful friendship: the widow in her seventies and her mother-in-law of eighty-five. They had forgotten a long period of time that had been filled with jealousy, rancor, and hatred. The deceased had been able to judge justly between people but had been unable to provide justice between his mother and his wife. He had also been unable to avoid taking sides. The man had departed and, for the first time, the two women had collaborated in something: the deep grief they felt for him.

Old age had tempered defiance and had opened windows to the breezes of wisdom.

The mother-in-law now prays for the widow and her offspring from the depths of her heart, for their health and long life, while the widow asks God to lengthen the life of the other woman lest she leave her alone and lonely.

Happiness

I returned to the old street after a long absence to attend a funeral.

No trace worth mentioning remained of its golden form.

On its two sides, towering buildings had replaced the villas, and it was crammed full of cars, dust, and turbulent waves of human beings.

With a feeling of great pride, I remembered its radiant appearance and the aroma of jasmine.

I remembered the beautiful girl who appeared at the window, casting her radiance on the passersby.

Who knows where lies her happy tomb in the city of the departed? There come to me now the words of the wise friend: "The first love is but a training that benefits the lucky ones who attain the love of God."

Music

He stood in my way, smiling and extending his hand. We shook hands as I asked myself who this old man could be. He took me to one side of the sidewalk.

"You've forgotten me?" he said.

In embarrassment I said, "Please forgive an old man's memory."

"We were neighbors when we were at primary school. In my spare time I used to sing to you in a beautiful voice, and you used to like those odes called *tawashih,* sung in praise of the Prophet."

Having totally despaired of me, he once again extended his hand.

"I mustn't delay you any further," he said.

I said to myself, "Such forgetfulness is like nonexistence! Rather, it is nonexistence itself. Yet I did and still do enjoy listening to *tawashih.*"

Exuberance

She looked at me with dull, lackluster eyes. The look expressed the bitterest suffering, yet the tongue was impotent.

I was visiting her in her illness. The room was empty.

Her skin was flabby, the bones sticking out.

Every corner was redolent of death.

O woman of unforgettable merrymaking.

My childhood was furnished with your delightful merry-making.

No fault was found in you other than that you were immoderately exuberant.

Yes indeed, immoderately exuberant.

A Message

I came across a dry rose, its petals scattered, behind a row of books as I was tidying up my library.

I smiled. The depths of the remote past gave way to a fleeting light.

And there freed itself from Time's grasp a feeling of nostalgia that lived for five minutes.

A fragrance that was like a whispering escaped from the dry petals.

I recalled the words of the wise friend: "The cruelty of the memory manifests itself in remembering what is dispelled in forgetfulness."

Reproof

I wander about aimlessly, bearing betrayal's thrust between my ribs.

The wise friend said that I was not the first to endure being abandoned. I asked him, "Has not old age a sacred standing?"

To which he said, "Deluded is he who is in love with some repeated old story."

I stood beneath the eucalyptus tree, gazing from afar at the place of entertainment, while she sat in the middle of the balcony. The clear light of allurement radiated from her: old age would not overtake her, nor would decay befall her.

She traverses me with a heedless glance, for her decision knows no alteration, and I shall return alone as I began.

A Lesson Learned

I sat in the large tent waiting for the funeral cortege to get under way. Above us reigned the memories of that faraway epoch.

The men from that time came walking one behind the other.

The earth used to tremble when any of them took a step.

Today they are old, lost men, remembered by no one.

Their successors came and the ground bent under their tread.

Their determined looks show they have taken possession of the earth and time.

At last the bier, borne upon shoulders, came into view, and everyone proceeded to depart.

The Important Post

At last I found myself being received by his office manager. I had arrived by dint of great effort and the intercession of people of note.

Giving a final glance at the recommendations I had submitted, he said, "The people intervening on your behalf are worthy of every consideration, but the test here is the only thing that matters."

"I am only too ready to be tested," I said urgently.

"I wish you success."

"When shall I be required to take the examination?" I asked eagerly.

"And why this particular post," he asked me, ignoring my own question, "when it demands such extraordinary effort?"

"Out of sheer love of it," I answered sincerely.

He smiled and made no comment.

As I was returning, I recalled the words of my wise friend: "He who owns life and willpower is the possessor of everything, and the poorest living creature owns life and willpower."

Living Pictures

This old picture brings together the members of my family, and this other one is of friends from long ago.

I looked at them both for so long that I sank into memories of the past.

All the faces were cheerfully radiant and at ease, eloquent with life.

There was no hint, not the slightest, of what lay hidden in the unknown.

And now they had all passed on, not a single one remained.

Who can determine that happiness was a living reality and not a dream or an illusion?

Justice

I went unhesitatingly to a well-known lawyer. How splendid was his frankness when he said to me, "You are in the right, but the opposing party is also in the right."

"I proposed to him," I said, "that we should seek the decision of some person in whom we both had confidence."

"There's no hope of finding such a person in this day and age!"

"I have registered letters which will convince the court of my honesty."

"They may be challenged as being forged."

"The fact is that I'm one hundred percent innocent."

"There's no one who is one hundred percent innocent."

"It's not impossible."

"Did you not, in a moment of anger, threaten to kill
him?"

"He didn't take what I said seriously."

"But he took many precautions, paid visits to various
shrines, and made solemn pledges."

I burst out laughing. "That was madness."

"It is up to you to prove he's mad, especially as his lawyer
will on his part try to prove that it's you who are mad."

My peals of laughter were interrupted by the lawyer:
"There's nothing to laugh about."

"To accuse me of madness is enough to make one
laugh."

"Rather, it induces sorrow."

"And why is that, sir?"

"Madness induces sorrow."

"Seeing that I'm in my right senses, the accusation is not
relevant."

"But being concerned may in itself mean madness."

"Are you in any doubt about my state of mind?" I asked
in consternation.

"Indeed, I am convinced—your inveterate disagreement
indicates that you are *both* mad."

"And yet you showed yourself quite prepared to defend
me?"

"It's my duty."

The lawyer gave a deep-seated sigh and continued. "And
don't forget I'm as mad as both of you."

From History

In that faraway time it was said that he had emigrated or fled. The fact was that he was sitting on the grass on the Nile bank wrapped around in the rays of the moon, conversing with his dreams in the presence of sublime beauty. At midnight he heard a slight movement in the surrounding silence. He saw the head of a woman emerging from the water right in front of where he was stretched out. He found himself before such beauty as he had not previously known. Could it possibly be someone rescued from some sunken vessel? But she was extremely sweet and serene, and he was seized by fear. He was about to rise to his feet and withdraw when she said to him in a gentle voice, "Follow me."

"Where to?" he asked, his fear increasing.

"Into the water, so that you may see your dreams with your own eyes."

With magical strength he advanced toward the water, his eyes not moving from her face.

The Specters

After performing the dawn prayers, I went wandering about in the empty streets. How pleasant it is to walk in the quietness and pure air, accompanied by the breezes of autumn. Having reached the heights above the desert, I seated myself on the rock known as "the Lad's Mother" and let my gaze wander in the desolate wilderness garbed in the delicate darkness. Suddenly it seemed that specters were moving toward the city. I told myself they must be, policemen, but then the first of them passed right in front of me and I made out a skeleton, with sparks flying from the sockets of its eyes. I was seized by terror as I sat there on the rock and the specters flowed past me, one after the other.

Trembling, I pondered what the day could be harboring for my slumbering city.

The Train of the Unexpected

At the spring festival it is pleasant to amuse oneself.

We stood, a group of pupils, in our shorts in the station hallway, each holding a colored straw basket filled with the food we had been given. We had to choose between two trips and two trains: one that went to the Barrages, and the other that went to an unknown destination and was called the Train of the Unexpected.

"The Barrages are beautiful and we know them," said one of us.

"Venturing into the unknown is more enjoyable," said another.

We could not come to a decision, so most of us went on the train to the Barrages. A few headed for the unknown.

Hammam al-Sultan

Once I dreamed that I was coming out of Hammam al-Sultan, the famous bathhouse in al-Gamaliyya. A young slave girl came up to me and invited me to meet her mistress. She took me along to her room to prepare me for the meeting, as her duty required of her. The training with her so distracted me from my goal that I almost forgot it. When I was required to go to the beautiful woman, I went feeling very embarrassed. I stood before her, defeated and overwhelmed by a feeling of collapse.

Thus the dream was transformed into a nightmare.

A miracle was needed for the sun to shine anew.

The Penalty

He saw him standing there in front of him like fate. He disappeared for a long time, but he did not bow to him or soften his gaze. With the speed of an earthquake, the string of gory memories was set in motion. He drew behind him the picture of his innocent family, who had known him as a model of industry and of the honest gaining of one's livelihood, ignorant of what lay behind that.

"We agreed to part for good."

"Necessity has its own laws and I am threatened with bankruptcy," said the visitor calmly. He told himself that the flood of pilfering begins with a drop.

"We were partners, so what befalls me also befalls you."

The visitor said, "When in despair I say, 'On me so on my enemies, O Lord.' "

It was his family that concerned him, even if suicide was the solution.

The Chance of a Lifetime

I happened to come across her sitting under a sunshade, watching her grandson building sand castles on the shore of the Mediterranean.

We greeted each other warmly and I seated myself at her side: two sedate old people under the umbrella of old age. Suddenly she laughed and said, "There's no point in being bashful at our age, so let me tell you an old story."

She told her story and I followed it with dismay. When she had finished, I said, "The chance of a lifetime missed— what a pity!"

How Impossible!

She never held back from me anything lovely that she possessed, for I imbibed from the spring of beauty until I had quenched my thirst. But ungrateful exultation in that with which one has been blessed may assume the mask of discontent, and one of the signs of my frustration was that I was joyful at parting. In the course of the long path I took, regret did not leave me, and even today her skeleton gazes at me in scorn.

An Unwritten Letter

In the same year I learned of Hammam's appointment as head of the court of appeals of Alexandria and read the news of the execution of Sayyid al-Ghadban for murdering a dancer. The three of us—Hammam, al-Ghadban, and I—had been childhood friends. Al-Ghadban had been the center of attention because of his beautiful voice and scabrous anecdotes. We had parted before reaching the age of nine and each had gone his separate way. I learned from some relatives that Hammam had gone into the judiciary, while I followed the news of al-Ghadban in the artistic press as a bouncer in a nightclub.

In truth, the news of his execution shook me and carried me off to reflecting on times past. I thought of writing a letter to Hammam expressing my feelings and thoughts. I began writing it, but then I stopped, for my enthusiasm had waned, thinking that he would have forgotten those times and those people, or that he was no longer concerned about such emotions.

The Last Visit

Were it not for Master Abd al-Da'im, every new-comer to the old city would have lost his way. He would meet them at the Muizz Café, of which he was the owner, and would then open all doors to them.

Abdallah was one of those newcomers. Master Abd al-Da'im had soon found him a job as an assistant doorkeeper, and Abdallah thanked his Lord for giving him his daily bread and shelter. He urged him to behave himself properly until he married him off to a decent girl. Abdallah began paying him visits at the café from time to time in acknowl-edgment of generous favors. But when he became wholly engrossed in work and bringing up his children, his visits became less frequent, until they ceased altogether. The man tasted life, the sweet and the bitter, and bore it patiently until the children were standing on their own feet and had all taken themselves off.

As he grew older, Abdallah felt that the time had come for him to take things easy and to spare himself any more worries. In his quiet time he remembered Master Abd al-Da'im and experienced a feeling of shame and regret; he made the decision to pay him a visit and prayed to God that he might find him in the best of health. He set off for the Muizz Café, having prepared his apologies and excuses. From the first glance he saw what had befallen the café in the way of renovation and the Westernized furnishings, service, and customers. He found no trace of its owner, and it was clear that no one had heard of him.

An old man appeared, wandering around with prayer

beads and incense. He was the only one who remembered Master Abd al-Da'im, the only one who knew his house in the Imam district. He knew no more about him than that. These difficulties did not prevent Abdallah from trying to accomplish his wish, so he went at once to the Imam, led by a strong feeling of loyalty and the sense that he was going someplace from which there was no return.

Layla

In the days of the struggle of ideas and radiant sun, Layla sparkled in an aura of beauty and allurement.

Some people said that she was a liberated pioneer, others that she was nothing but an immoral woman.

When the sun set and the struggle and the ideas disappeared from sight in the shadows, many emigrated to the far corners.

Years later they returned, each armed with a purse of gold and a cargo of disrepute. Layla laughed loud and long and inquired derisively, "I wonder what you have to say now about immorality?"

Mercy

The house was old, also the man and wife.

He was in his sixties, she in her seventies.

They were brought together by love thirty years ago, then

it had abandoned them along with the rest of their expectations.

Had it not been for their state of destitution, the bird would have fled the cage. He was always afflicted with a voracity for life, while she suffered from excessive timidity.

He would console his waking dreams by buying lottery tickets, harboring vague hopes. Whenever he bought a ticket he would mumble, "Your compassion, O Lord."

The woman's heart would tremble with terror, and she would mumble: "Your compassion, O Lord."

The Search

At evening he set off for the burial ground where he used to congregate with some of his comrades to pass the evening in lighthearted chatter and to exchange moans of complaint.

"How did your efforts turn out today?" one of them asked him.

"As on previous days," he answered listlessly.

"You're wasting your time with good-for-nothings," said another, "while we've got the shortest path to prosperity."

"And the shortest path to prison as well," he said with annoyance.

To which another said derisively, quoting the Qur'an, "God changes nothing in a people until they change themselves."

Question and Answer

The old man asked the woman, "Pardon me, my lifelong friend, but why do you expend yourself on the insignificant?"

Dumbfounded, she answered, "I owe it to you to tell the truth frankly. I used to sell love at a handsome profit, and I came to buy it at considerable loss. I have no other choice with this wicked and fascinating life."

The Challenge

In the flood of a political dispute a deputy asked a minister, "Can you show me a person who is clean and unsullied?"

The minister answered challengingly, "You need but one example of many—children, the idiotic, and the mad—and the world's still doing fine."

The Millieme

I found myself as a child wandering uncertainly in the street. In my hand I had a millieme, but I had completely forgotten what my mother had told me to buy. I tried to bring it to memory but failed. I was nonetheless certain that what I had gone out to buy did not cost more than a millieme.

Tears of Laughter

I said to him, "Thanks be to God, you have carried out your mission to the full, brought your family to dry land, and so ripped out the rapacious fangs from the monster of time. So the time has come for you to relax in peace in the few days that remain."

He glared at me with suspicion and asked, "Do you remember our pure days in early times?"

Reading his misgivings, I said, "Those times are over and past."

In a confessional tone he said, "My one and only friend, at the height of triumph and prosperity often did I weep for esteem that had been lost."

Dialogue

The father returned to the house and found his sons awaiting him.

He took out his wallet and muttered, "The father in this age of ours is a martyr."

At which they kept silent.

Then the martyrs dispersed.

The Beggar

He swims in the sea of the past and is submerged by a wave tinged with a dark color, its echo spreading out in a sorrowful melody that does not vanish. When a man is in his twenties and the woman next to him is over fifty, she bestows upon him memories of tender motherhood. In an innocent seclusion, thoughts from the world of burning desires make their appearance, and the fever heat of the call shows up in the sparkle of the eye.

Shyness bridles him for a while, accompanied by something like fear. After that comes regret, and he begs for forgetfulness.

Loneliness

The ugly scene clung to her memory and would not be shifted: the scene of the officer's blind slap as it landed on the cheek of her sick father. As much as she used to love her father and revere him, so did she dispute everything, herself, and the world around her. She grew old alone, watched with pity by the universe.

The Birthday

How aimlessly he goes his way. When fatigue overcomes him he stops, but he does not cease conversing secretly with things stationary and moving.

At the end of this year he will be thirty years of age.

A Question After Thirty Years

After being separated for twenty years from the quarter of my youth, chance caused me to pass through it. Were it not for the slumbering emotions that boiled within me I would not have recognized it, with its new buildings and noisy crowds. My eyes came to rest on an old house that had retained its former state, and I felt a smile flickering on soul and body. Today, in her eighties, she is alone. The last time we had met by chance was thirty years ago, when she informed me that her only son was going abroad permanently. I folded up my umbrella and, after some hesitation, went to the door and pressed the bell. The partly opened door revealed the face of a woman who was a stranger, so I concealed my confusion by asking, "Doesn't Mrs. Samia live here?"

"We've been living here for three years," she answered at once.

I turned around in embarrassment and went on my way,

asking myself where she could possibly be. Was she living in some other quarter? Had she joined her son abroad? Had she departed from this world of ours without our knowing, even though we were related? Was this a suitable ending to that history that blazed with emotions and dreams?

During the same year I was brought together at a funeral with the rest of the family, so I asked one of them, "What do you know of Mrs. Samia?"

He raised his eyebrows in astonishment and said, "I believe she's still living in the old house!"

A Face from the Past

I saw Sitt Naffousa in a dream.

What brought you after an absence of seventy years, or even more? Your appearance was splendid, your complexion clear, your hair luxuriant. Your house used to overlook the Nile. We used to visit you often; I consider the times we visited you among the happiest. From your bedroom window I would immerse my gaze in the calm waves, and it would float across to the far shore.

Nothing has remained of the dream but your face and the question I ask myself: "Is she still alive?"

As for the events of the dream, they vanished as soon as I awoke.

The Rain

The rain drove us into the entrance of an old house. Outside was the sound of the pelting rain and the rumbling of thunder, while inside was the color of sunset.

We stood opposite one another in the narrow entrance, with nothing but the stairwell and our secret thoughts. I said to myself, "What a woman!"—while she gazed out at the cold weather, proudly reticent.

As though talking to herself, she said, "This rain's a real nuisance!"

Confused by my thoughts, I said, "It's a mercy for mankind."

The Man with a Watch

He is always close to me. He never leaves my sight or my imagination, a sparkle in his strong, calm glances. From a neutral face, he shares with me neither joy nor sadness. From time to time he looks at his watch, suggesting to me that I do the same. Sometimes I grow weary of him, but if he is away for a moment I am overcome by a sense of loss. All the fatigue or comfort I have met with in my life has been of his making. And it is he who made me yearn for a life in which no clock strikes the hours.

The Sorceress

It passed by me in my seclusion like a budding rose on its verdant stalk. The memories of those dazzling days rained down and I was aghast at the speed of time. I had complained to my wise friend about some of what I had experienced, and he commented, "Do you deny that you had your share of the warmth of the world and its fragrance?"

So I counted the blessings I had received as an affirmation of the favors of the Bestower, and he said, "All these instances of good fortune are the fruit of its turning its back on you."

After a short silence he asked me, "Do you not remember being excited at it when it came to you?"

"A fleeting look of contentment under the date palm!" I said.

"Do you remember the taste of it?"

"More delicious than all the instances of good fortune put together."

To which he said gently, "So it is that I say to you that it is the secret of life and its light."

Opening the Way

I was waiting close to the wall on the narrow road crammed with people and shops. At that time I was tormented by a sense of loss and being driven by conflicting winds. Some hidden force drew me to one side, and I saw a venerable old man approaching me, diffusing a serene goodness. When he was right up close to me he whispered, "It's not worth a thing."

I was convinced that he had read my inner thoughts and that he was inviting me to cut all ties. I trembled in all my limbs and my heart thumped.

Temptation manifested itself to me in the shape of a lovely woman of such beauty as I had never seen before. But I hesitated, and in that very instant my wife returned carrying the paper bags of spices and herbs and trailing behind her my three sons.

I wakened from my momentary lapse and took up the youngest in my arms, and my family opened up for itself a way through the crowd.

The Man's Secret

He would pass by where we were sitting, shouting, "It is coming, of that there is no doubt."

Then he would rush off, nothing remaining of him except for the image of his ragged clothes and distracted look.

And the catastrophe did come to pass.

Some people said that he was a saint, others that he was nothing but a secret agent.

A Man Reserves a Seat

The bus started on its journey from Zeytoun at the same moment that a private car set forth from the owner's house in Helwan. Each varied the speed at which it was traveling, speeding along and then slowing down, and perhaps coming to a stop for a minute or more depending on the state of the traffic.

They both, however, reached Station Square at the same time, and even had a slight accident, in which one of the bus's headlights was broken and the front of the car was scratched.

A man was passing and was crushed between the two vehicles and died. He was crossing the square in order to book a seat on the train going to Upper Egypt.

A Gift

In the solitude and frailty of old age, contemplation spreads like the aroma of incense. He said to his friend who devoted himself to worship, as though apologizing, "With the pressing concerns of my family and the demands of things generally, my life was squandered and I didn't find the time for worship."

That night he was visited in his dreams by someone who made him a present of a white rose and whispered in his ear, "A gift that is deserved only by sincere worshipers!"

The Golden Tomb

I saw in my dream a golden tomb standing under the branches of a lofty tree covered with singing nightingales. On its front was written in beautifully clear letters: "Happy is he whose upbringing was in the crucible of being abandoned."

The Note

One day I came across a rose lying on the ground at my feet. There was something particularly attractive about it, so I picked it up and found that a folded slip of paper had been tied with white thread around its green stalk. Curious, I spread it out and read: "Come. I shall be as you would like to find me."

I thought the matter over with a smile and asked myself how it was that the note had not reached its destination. Why had it been thrown into the dirt?

For a time I roamed in the valley of suppositions and probabilities, but I gave praise to a world in which the source of love never dries up.

Breezes from the distant past blew upon me, my heart beat as wildly as it was able, and suddenly I relinquished my old hesitation.

I resolved to commence taking steps to secure a place of burial for myself in this vast city.

The Call

Sometimes he appears to me with his handsome face. He gives me a gentle look and whispers, "Leave everything and follow me."

He may meet me when I am in a state of extreme frustration or in the utmost happiness, and always he snatches from my breast amusement and rebellion.

And neither of us has yet known despair.

The Hoped-For Promise

With the adversities of old age, isolation, and speculations from which rosewater drips, the breaths of the hoped-for promise resound.

Unexpectedly, the bell rang and the neighbor came asking permission to enter.

She immersed herself in that in which I was immersed to such an extent that I believed her to be the hoped-for promise.

Plunging into the Water

One night he witnessed the eclipse of the moon. From his misery that was concealed behind the dark veil, he drew a feeling of depression that cut him off from things.

He was no longer delighted by anything, and the doctors were at a loss. He was advised to emigrate to some faraway place, to change his surroundings and routine. In despair he went wandering about on the seashore. At a distance he saw a parasol under which stretched out a half-naked woman, who was exceedingly beautiful and composed. He was drawn toward her as the first thing he met that did not evoke within him a feeling of sadness and gloom. He felt that she was welcoming him, without a word or a movement, and he was carried away with joy. She rose and made for the water, so he stripped himself of his clothes and followed her. They dived into the water together without casting a single glance behind them.

Repentance

The beautiful, attractive woman passed by me, sighing and with swaying gait, and I paid her no attention.

In that dry time I took pleasure in the gratification of the pride of abstinence and of shunning worldly temptations.

On a radiantly moonlit night I rushed at a bound to my true nature and sped after this beautiful, attractive woman, apprehensive of being rebuked for having shunned her, but she received me with a smile and said, "Be happy in your fate, for I accept repentance."

The Glorification of God

In broad daylight, with the alley teeming with its inhabitants—men, women, and children—and with the shops on both sides ready to receive customers—in broad daylight, a weak man fell victim to a giant of a man. The people saw the crime and hid themselves away in the tower of fear.

Not one of them testified, and the murderer got off scot-free.

The dervish witnessed the incident, but he was not asked about it because it was firmly believed that he was simpleminded. The simpleminded man was enraged, so he made up his mind to take revenge on everybody. Whenever the opportunity came his way, he would do away with a man or woman—while singing the praises of God.

Advice

We had a neighbor who was the novice of a Sufi sheikh. He would invite his sheikh every Thursday night to hold a session of chanting and reciting the names of God.

I was standing with the boys behind those who had been invited and who were squatting on rugs.

We were enraptured by the reciting and the chanting.

Once, one of the disciples said to the sheikh, "We see that you have a smart appearance and are clearly in the best of health. You like food and drink and are not like those abstinent sheikhs."

The sheikh answered in a voice that was heard by everyone, "We are people who work for our daily bread and do not beg. We occupy ourselves with God's world and do not shun it. Our delight is in the ardor of love and spiritual intoxication. Our nightly journeying is in contemplation and recitation."

The Lesson

I was rushing off to attend the session of recitation. On my way I passed by an old man raggedly dressed, of wretched appearance, who was weeping. I paid him no attention, lest I miss my appointment.

When the sheikh took his place in the middle of the circle of recitation, he looked around him until his gaze fell on me. He motioned to me to approach, then leaned over my ear and whispered, "You ignored the old man who was weeping and you missed an opportunity for doing good, the likes of which you won't obtain by listening to my lesson today."

The Night of Power[*]

We decorated the reception room with roses, and the smell of incense flowed out from the windows of our house into the middle of the street. We did everything we could to give pleasure to the ear and eye. Our hope, like that of others, was that the sheikh would be our guest and spend the Night of Power with us. My father became engrossed in reading from the Qur'an, and I began going back and forth between the window and the open door. Suddenly in the sublimity of the night there rang out trilling cries of joy from a neighbor's house.

Said my father with a deep sigh, "Good luck no longer wants to smile."

A Whisper at Dawn

At a decisive stage of life, when love brought me to the highest peaks of confusion and longing, there whispered in my ear a voice at dawn: "Congratulations to you— the time for making your farewells has been decreed."

Deeply affected, I closed my eyes and saw my funeral moving along, with myself at its head carrying a large glass filled with the nectar of life.

---

[*] The night in the month of Ramadan in which the Qur'an was first revealed.

Leaving

Only at his funeral did I really feel that he had died. The chairs were occupied by people offering their condolences, and this was followed by a recital from the Holy Qur'an. All those sitting next to each other engaged in conversation, and innumerable stories were told. They concerned everybody except the deceased, who was mentioned by no one. Dear one, truly you departed from this world to the Mighty One as though it had departed from you.

The Dull-Witted Woman

The servant was dull-witted; they called her "the Sheikha." Lady Waheeda was in her sixties. The house was sometimes disrupted by the force of desire. The feeling of disruption invaded the soul of the dull-witted servant, and she was overcome by a state of melancholy. Sympathetically the lady asked her, "What's wrong, Sheikha?"

"I'm leaving," she answered huffily.

The lady of the house was upset and asked, "Are you going to leave me on my own, Sheikha?"

"You're not on your own, you brazen hussy," she said sharply.

The Pure

As the Sheikha walked in the market in her white gal-labiya and green head covering, she saw a man at his wit's end.

"What are you looking for, man?" she asked him.

At the end of his patience, he answered, "I am looking for some pure water."

In a tone of voice that was not without rebuke, she said, "You will find nothing more pure than the sweat of a woman."

Life

The circumstances of life obliged me one day to be a brigand. I first practiced my profession one dark night when I pounced on a wayfarer. The man was so terrified that he almost died. With fervent entreaty, he called out, "Take everything I possess as yours, but don't harm my life."

From that moment on I have been hovering with my soul around the secret of life!

The Blessed Memory

My wise friend asked me about an unforgettable dream and I said:

I found myself in a tavern amid a group of good and blessed people who were drinking and singing. Someone asked, "Who's the lucky one?"

The curtain hanging down over the door of the tavern was pushed aside and there entered a naked woman with the bloom of the nectar of life and its charm.

We stood in wonder, looking and waiting. The woman moved toward me until she was right next to me. She undid the knot of her braided hair and it spilled around us like an unruly wave until it covered us.

All of us were intoxicated with an all-enveloping happiness, and we all sang out together, "Glad tidings to us—we have attained the objects of our desires."

In the Spacious Room

In the dream I saw myself in a spacious, high-ceilinged room, devoid of all furniture except for a round table in the middle, with two chairs around it facing each other. I sat on one chair and a close friend of mine sat on the other. In front of each of us was a cup of coffee. There was a door leading into another room which was extremely dark and I knew nothing of what was inside it.

"We must carry out the task," my friend said.

"We really must carry it out," I agreed.

Suddenly my friend rose, moved toward the dark room, and disappeared. After he had left I noticed that the coffee was no longer on the table, so I called out to him. I heard no reply, but a stranger appeared and sat down in his place. His white cloak attracted my attention. Although I did not know him, I told myself that his presence there was better than not. Placing a glass in front of himself and another in front of me, he said, "Let us drink the toast of light and dark."

So I raised the cup to drink. I happened to glance inside it and saw the face of my absent friend staring at me. My hand shook and I said to the man sitting in front of me, "We must carry out the task."

The Tune

In another dream I found myself in a medium-sized room lit by a gas lamp hanging from the ceiling. In a corner a group of men and women sat on cushions facing one another, conversing and laughing in loud voices. There was neither door nor window in the walls apart from a small opening the size of a peephole, placed rather high up. Through it I could see only a sky concealing itself behind the evening. I felt a strong desire to go back to my home and my people. I did not know how this would be made possible for me. I asked the people engaged in conversation, "May the good Lord bless you, how can I leave here?"

No one paid any attention to me, and they continued

talking and laughing. I was upset at my deep loneliness. Then, through the opening, there appeared a face with indistinct features. It said to me, "Here is this tune. Learn it from me well and sing it when required, and you will find in it the cure for every worry and affliction."

Temptation

I was strolling past the green doorway leading to the tomb when I came across a dervish who was moving to one side with a woman. She was of middle age, exuding femininity, with a plump body, and a bashful disposition.

As I approached them, I heard her say, "Sir, I am a widow and I live with my sister. Thanks be to God, I am chaste, but I am frightened of temptation."

"Perform the obligatory prayers," he told her.

"Not a prayer do I miss," she said with sincerity. "And I listen to the reciting of the Qur'an at every opportunity."

"The Devil will not touch you," he said.

"But I am frightened of temptation," she said.

The Battle

I went back to the square after visiting the shrine of al-Husayn. I saw a crowd staring at a dancer and a man playing a pipe. The piper was making music and the dancer was swaying and playing with a stick, while the people clapped and faces shone with rapturous happiness. I thought angrily of ways I could disperse the gathering, but in a moment of light I saw all of them in God's good time, as they hurried toward the grave. It was as though they were racing one another, until not one of them remained.

At that I turned my back on them and went off.

The Lights

The camera was made ready in its place, the lights were adjusted, and the director gave the signal for shooting to begin.

Two lovers met and there was some dialogue. The shooting of the scene came to an end.

The distributor whispered to the producer as they sat at an easy distance behind the camera.

"She won't be any good for romantic parts after today. I feel sorry for her."

The actress lit a cigarette to calm her nerves after the stress of acting.

The writer stood in a corner far from the lights, listening and following, no one paying him any attention.

At the Table
of the Merciful One*

The table of the Merciful One was peopled with those who were fasting. When the sound of the call to prayers reached them, they made ready and invoked the name of God. A man of importance called out, "Our food is forbidden to him in whose heart there is any wrong."

A loud laugh escaped from a man at whom all eyes were directed.

He stopped laughing and said, "I have lovelier food, so listen to me."

But they set about the food, as they made fun of the man.

When all stomachs were filled, eyes grew heavy and they took a short nap. In their sleep they saw a world that was fascinating and magical. When they woke up they turned toward the man who had laughed and found no trace of him.

The absent man left a feeling of anguish in every heart.

---

*During the fasting month of Ramadan, rich people often set up tables in the streets where the poor can break their fast at sunset; these are known as "tables of the Merciful One."

Billiards

I seated myself in the corner of the café with a billiard table. An energetic man came along and began playing against himself, taking turn and turn about.

I said to him politely, "Would you allow me to play you? It's more fun."

Without looking at me, he said, "For me the fun is playing on my own and having others watch."

I looked around and saw that all the customers were fast asleep.

The Pearl

Someone came to me in a dream and held out an ivory box, saying, "Accept the gift."

When I woke up the box was on the pillow.

I opened it in a daze and found a pearl the size of a hazelnut.

From time to time I would show it to a friend or an expert and ask him, "What do you think of this incomparable pearl?"

The man would shake his head and say with a laugh, "What pearl? The box is empty."

I would be astonished at his denial of what was there before my eyes.

Up until now I have found no one who would believe me, and yet despair has never made its way into my heart.

The Coincidence

Under the statue we met by chance.

I came to a stop: he was smiling and I was thrown into confusion. I shook his hand with the deference he deserved, and he asked me, "How are you?"

I answered politely, shyly. "Thanks be to God—your kindness is not forgotten."

He said, in a voice that was not devoid of a gentle rebuke, "It's good to depend on yourself, but it seems to me that you have forgotten me."

I said shyly, "I don't wish to be a burden to you, but you are wholly indispensable."

We parted, my apprehensions aroused. I remembered the long time I had been in contact with him, when he was everything in my life; I also recollected his kindness and his favors. I remembered, too, his other traits, such as his avoidance of me, his sternness, and his lack of concern without giving any explanation that might reassure one's heart.

Despite everything, I regarded the meeting as a happy coincidence.

Longing

I used to meet him in the open air, alone, conversing with the flute, making music to the splendor of the universe.

I said to him one day, "How appropriate that people should hear your tunes."

To which he said with displeasure, "They are engrossed in quarreling and lamentation."

"Everyone," I said encouragingly, "has a moment when he longs for the open air."

Obedience

During her life she never refused a request or ignored a gesture.

She used to answer the call of passion without heeding the price.

Someone warned her of the bad outcome.

But she had a strong belief in the Merciful, the Compassionate.

The Hour of Reckoning

He sat eating his food in the small restaurant, quietly and with appetite, not well dressed and with drained features.

When the time came for paying the bill, he said to the owner of the restaurant, "Please forgive me, but I don't have a single millieme in my pocket. I was dying of hunger."

The man was amazed and did not know what to do, but he was careful to keep the incident a secret so that no one would know.

Negligence

Like sparrows frolicking under the wing of their parents. The house was small and their living conditions were circumscribed, but they could conceive of no felicity to surpass the one they enjoyed. One of the scorching days of summer, with its breaths laden with humidity, went on and on, at which a sparrow called out, "Ugh, when will autumn come?"

Gazing at them from afar, he mumbled, "Why do you waste the good days that are granted you?"

A Trick of the Memory

I saw an enormous person with a stomach as large as the ocean, and a mouth that could swallow an elephant.

I asked him in amazement, "Who are you, sir?"

He answered with surprise, "I am forgetfulness. How could you have forgotten me?"

Eloquence

The professor said, "Eloquence is magic."

So, believing his words, we began vying with one another in quoting examples.

Then my imagination took me to a faraway past, where it roamed innocently.

I brought to mind simple words of no importance in themselves, like: "You . . . what are you thinking about? . . . Fine. . . . Oh, what a crafty person you are."

And yet through their strange inscrutable magic people have gone mad, while others have become intoxicated with indescribable happiness.

Rapture

What a time, the time of rapture! Golden throats send forth their melodies, spreading their fragrance like a delicious, penetrating aroma.

A beautiful woman circles around the halo of the music, loved by pure-white hearts. But no trace is found of her other than in the world of music. She has chosen the heart of music as a site for herself that she never leaves.

On the Shore

I found myself on a strip of land separating the sea from the desert. I had a feeling of isolation that was close to fear. In a moment my bewildered glance alighted upon a woman neither far away nor close by. I could not make out her features and lineaments clearly, but I was seized with the hope that I would find that in some way she was related or acquainted. I went toward her, but the distance between us did not lessen and gave no hope of reaching her. I called out to her, using a number of names and numerous descriptions, but she did not stop, did not turn around.

Evening came and all created things began to vanish, yet I did not cease to look around, to walk, or to call out.

The Secret of Intoxication

I dreamed that I had woken from a deep sleep to the gentle breathing of a woman who was a paragon of beauty. She cast a sweet look at me and whispered in my ear, "He who has lodged in me the secret of creative rapture is capable of everything, so never despair."

Dazzlement

It was widely reported that he was knowledgeable about everything. Groups of people went to him at the corner of the street where he sat on a couch. A well-meaning mediator said, "There is no time for simple questions. Let's have some really tough ones."

He was assailed with some truly tough questions. A deep silence reigned so that everyone might hear the answer that would succor him. I saw no movement of his lips and heard no sound issuing from his mouth.

I came away from his presence amid groups of people dazzled to the point of frenzy by what they had heard.

The Recollection

O n market day in our alley there wended through the throngs of people a naked woman with a swinging gait. She was walking with head held high, with charms fit to melt the very stones. The people ceased buying and selling, and stood with dazed eyes. Thus she went on until she was hidden from view by the final bend. The people awoke from their bewilderment and were overcome by a state of frenzy. They rushed toward the bend. They searched everywhere, but found no trace of her. Every time the recollection of her came to their hearts they were consumed by grief.

Regret

B orne to me on the battling waves of life was a woman. No sooner did I see her than my heart was stirred with the memories of youth. When the confusion of meeting melted in the fire of memories, I asked her, "Do you remember?"

She gave a faint smile that substituted for an answer.

So I said rashly, "Remembering must precede regret."

"How do you find it?" she asked me.

"Painful, like yearning," I said passionately.

She gave a soft laugh, then whispered, "That is so—and God is Merciful, Compassionate."

The Battle

At the time of youthfulness and little patience, a quarrel broke out between me and a friend. A flood of anger swamped the affection there had been between us, and he challenged me to a fight in the open air where there would be no one to separate us. We went off all prepared. We were soon engaged in a fierce battle that went on until we fell down from exhaustion, our wounds bleeding copiously.

We had to return to the city before nightfall. This we were unable to accomplish without helping each other. We each had to assist the other in tending to our wounds; we also needed each other's assistance in walking.

During our stumbling progress, our hearts grew serene, and smiles appeared on swollen lips. Then forgiveness loomed on the horizon.

The Dialogue
of Late Afternoon

He is our neighbor—and what a fine neighborhood, what a splendid neighbor!

In the late afternoon he sits cross-legged on a couch in front of the door, enveloped in his cloak.

Thus the square achieves its full majesty and the trees their full beauty. When the sky bids farewell to the last kite, his three sons return from their work. On the evening before traveling to the Pilgrimage, he looked into their faces and asked, "What do you say after what has happened?"

The eldest answered, "There's no hope without the law."

The middle one answered, "There is no life without love."

The youngest answered, "Justice is the basis of the law and of love."

The father smiled and said, "It is necessary to have a certain amount of anarchy in order for the unmindful to awake from his state of indifference."

The brothers exchanged a long look, then said in one breath, "You are always right."

The Journey

Through a destiny over which I had no power, I had to
submit to being away from my homeland. I realized that
the event would come about without any doubt, either tomorrow or the day after.

Wait a little and do not anticipate the unknown.

The good-hearted said: Don't be afraid, for we have
been along the same path before you.

There spreads out before me a garden filled with beauty,
with enchanting women going to and fro.

I was invited to the singing, but it was as though I had
become preoccupied with thoughts and misgivings.

I rid myself of all sensation to cross the gory jungle.

All that remains to me of the crossing are the memories
of specters, the echoes of choking nightmares, and the lasting trace of a bloody battle.

They said the time had come for me to roam about in
the gardens of the north, but my heart took me to the play-
ground between the public fountain and the hospice.

I arrived, panting.

The face, the skin, the look. Everything had changed.

The loved ones met me, while around them there extended far into the distance the sublime with its special atmosphere and clamor.

My heart said to me: Settle in its shade, and may the
Eternal preserve it.

The Aroma

He looked behind him for a long time, and nothing remained of him but that which remains of the rose after it has dried.

Fun, untroubled dreams, and the warmth of the loving woman.

Always advanced in years, she is not permitted to grow old, and always she praises God in prayer.

After the darkness he was laid out, while the banner of parting was unfolded, the line of people bidding farewell moved on, and there came a sigh from the bridegroom whose marriage did not come about.

The faces of love vanished, and the air was redolent with a fragrant aroma.

The Constant and the Changing

They went to the market and I remained on in the house alone.

A young girl with two pigtails came. The scent of carnations wafted from her. She was carrying an empty dish, and had been sent by her mother on some special errand.

When she did not find my mother, she was about to leave, but I called to her to wait and she did so.

Those who were trading in the market all melted away,

and the sparrows chirruped for a long time, showing her the summer and hiding from her the winter. In order to fill the time I said to her, "It would be best for you to take off some of your clothes."

"When the right time of the year comes," she answered shyly.

And so the time and the place and longing brought us together.

As for the time and the place, they have no stability; and as for longing, it bequeaths nothing but sadness.

The Task

My mother said to me, "Go to our neighbor and tell her to bring the thing held in trust."

About to set off, I asked her, "And what does 'in trust' mean?"

Hiding a smile, she said, "Don't ask about something that is no concern of yours—but when you receive it, guard it as though it were your soul."

I went to our neighbor and gave her the message. She moved her limbs to drive away sluggishness and said, "You must see my house first."

She ordered me to follow her and went ahead of me with strutting gait.

Time passed like a flowing river.

My mother used sometimes to come to my mind, and I would imagine her as she waited.

In the Storm

My foot was slipping and sliding on a stormy, rainy night, so I took refuge in the shop of a druggist.

"When will the storm calm down?" I asked him.

"Maybe after a minute, and maybe it will go on until tomorrow evening."

By the light of the shop's lantern, I saw someone hurrying along outside with a black umbrella spread above his head.

I felt that I was not seeing him for the first time, although I did not know him. The fact was that I did not like the look of him. The druggist said to him, "One's not to blame if one prefers being safe and sound tonight."

Going on his way without stopping, the man said, "I never fail to keep an appointment."

A beautiful woman came to seek shelter at the shop, so we forgot the man and his umbrella.

It seems that the woman decided to take the opportunity to do some shopping, so she asked the druggist, "Have you some medicine for uneasy thoughts and insomnia?"

The man pointed at a jar.

"There is nothing in the world," he said, "lovelier than health and an unworried mind."

The Detective

I was preparing for bed when there was a knock at the door. I opened the peephole and saw the form of a man shutting off the space in front of my gaze.

"A detective from the police station," he said.

He stretched his hand out to me with a notice ordering me to come with him for some important matter.

It was usual in our quarter for this detective to go to a resident's home to give him a summons. He would go at any time and without observing any consideration, and there was nothing one could do but comply. I found it was futile to argue, so I went back to my bedroom to dress.

I walked at his heels without exchanging a single word.

In the windows I caught sight of the blurred shapes of people following us with their eyes and whispering together.

I know what they are whispering, for I had often done just that when following those who had gone before.

The Wind
Does As It Wishes

Time grew tired at the way I had treated it in the early days.

I made up my mind to live in peace and went to sleep.

But the wind that separates one from one's native land bore me off above the clouds, complying with the orders of the Unknown.

It was not my intention to do what I was doing, nor did I do what I intended.

My gentle friend ended his sleep and said, "Tomorrow we will impose by force our will on life."

Calling on the universe to be my witness, I said, "Let God's will prevail."

The Guide and the Vendor

From the first day I discovered that my work in the district required me to travel around continually in the area. I asked about a guide and they directed me to a man who lived in Darb al-Ahmar. I noticed that he was blind, but knowledgeable people assured me of his discernment and depth of experience, and said that he knew by heart all the corners of the quarter.

I took his arm under mine and he walked off with me with firm tread. I quickly had confidence in him and grew to like him. I could have stayed with him alone until the end of life, had it not been that one day we met by chance a pretty woman who sold bread. I therefore bade my farewell and went off with her. Sometimes along the way I would meet up with my old guide. Though I would greet him warmly, he would answer me with indifference, and we would each proceed on our way.

And perhaps in some free moments we would enjoy mentioning him in joking and fun, but it was out of the question that a man in his senses would deny his merit.

Give Yourself Up

He came to mind and my heart exploded with longing. I went to his home at the end of the suburban dwellings surrounded by fields. He gave me a friendly welcome and said, "A lifetime has passed since your last visit, but you have come at an appropriate time."

He said this as he pointed to a low table on which had been placed a tray of supper consisting of grilled fish, olives, and hot bread.

He invited me to share the meal, and I sat down.

We had scarcely said "In the name of God" when a voice from a loudspeaker came to us, calling out, "Give yourself up."

He jumped up to the light switch and turned it off, so that darkness reigned. Soon shots poured down upon us like rain from all directions.

Trembling with fear, I told myself, "Happy is he who can give himself up."

After You Come Out of Prison

The hall was packed with petitioners.

We sat down exchanging anxious looks and directing our gaze at the high door leading to the inside, which was covered with two halves of a giant green screen.

When would luck smile and my turn come? When would I be invited to the interview so that I could present my requirement and obtain hope? The door is open and turns away no one who goes to it, yet only the lucky ones achieve a meeting.

Thus the days proceed and I go with heart gladdened by hope, then return dejected.

A thought occurred to me: Why did I not disappear in some place in the garden until the evening party broke up and the man came out for his evening stroll, when I would throw myself at his feet. But the servants perceived that I had slipped in and they dragged me off to the police station, and from the police station to the prison, where I was cast into its darkness.

In vain did I attempt to clear myself.

How was it that I had gone aspiring to an honorable post and had ended up in prison?

Exchanged whisperings brought to our knowledge the fact that the important man would be visiting the prison and would investigate the conditions in it and listen to the complaints of those who had been unjustly treated.

I was astonished that I would achieve in prison what had been impossible for me in the outside world.

And this need of mine for his sympathy increased and grew more intense.

With bent head I told him my story.

He showed neither that he believed it nor that he disbelieved it.

"All that I wish," I said entreatingly, "is that I be allowed a meeting after I come out of prison."

About to depart, he said in a calm voice, "After you come out of prison."

The River

In the exuberant whirlpool of life we were gathered in a public place at one of the festivals.

Who is that old woman who stares at me with smiling eyes?

Perhaps the world had brought us together at some time.

Her smile widened, so I smiled, returning her greeting.

"Do you not remember?" she asked me.

My smile became wider.

She said with a forwardness that is only attained by old women, "You were the first experience I had while you were a student."

Silence reigned for a moment, then she said, "We were only a step away!"

I asked myself in bewilderment where that beautiful life had lost itself.

Conversation from Afar

In our alley there is a haunted house that no one goes near, for its door and windows are closed and it is given over to the forces of decay. I would pass it by and not believe my eyes. I would tell myself that it was nothing but one of the legends of old.

One day, passing in front of its door, I was caught unawares by the rain. I was holding it in scorn as usual when a voice gently reached me.

"If you are in any doubt, spend a night in the house and the proof will come to you without a medium."

I was seized by terror and became tongue-tied.

I remembered what I had read about the world of ghosts, at which the voice said, "Keep to the rational or else you'll be exposed to our cruel experience."

The rain grew more violent and the voice grew silent, as though it had dissolved into it.

A Very Young Philosopher

Despite myself and without any call, I was pursued by a sense of old age. I do not know how I could become oblivious of the approach of the end, the supremacy of leave-taking: a salute to the long life I had spent in safety and bliss, a salute to the enjoyment of life in the sea of tenderness, progress, and knowledge.

Now the eternal voice gives the call for departure. Bid your beautiful world farewell and go to the unknown. And the unknown, O heart of mine, is nothing but extinction. Put away the vain falsehoods of being transferred to another life. How, why, what rationale justifies its existence? The truly reasonable is what my heart sorrows over. Farewell, O life from which I have derived every meaning.

Then it ended, leaving behind a history devoid of any meaning.

(From the musings of a fetus at the end of its ninth month.)

The Fact of the Matter

The woman on the balcony gazes down from behind the latticework with eyes full of alertness and compassion. The small boy plays below the house and sings. From time to time he goes off to one of the lanes that empty out into the sides of the square coming from the vast areas of the city. At sunset the little boy tears himself away from the world of playing and roaming about, and enters the house.

Things do not stay like that for long.

The balcony is emptied of compassion.

And the little boy has penetrated deep into the lane, and has not come back.

The Man Who Made a Prediction

We were invited to an evening party at a friend's house. We sat around him in the small garden, intoxicated by the aroma of orange blossom, while our friend talked to us of a lucrative project in which we might participate. By the light of a match, I caught a glimpse of a colleague who was far away in a world of his own dreams. I jogged him with my elbow, but he did not turn toward me.

As we were going back, I said to him, "Certainly you didn't hear a word our friend said."

With provocative simplicity he said, "My heart told me that he would be leaving this world of ours before sunrise."

The extraordinary thing is that the man with the project did indeed die before the rising of the sun.

But even more extraordinary was the fact that the other friend, who had made the prediction, died at dawn.

From that day on, whenever time bestowed an agreeable hour, I refused to absent myself from it because of something that had passed or something that was to come.

The Heart's Complaint

My heart grew heavy after time had turned away from me. The doctor went on searching for the secret cause of its malady in the X ray. I contemplated it with curiosity until it seemed to me that it was seeing me as I saw it, and that we were exchanging looks. There also passed through its eyes a look of rebuke, so I said to it apologetically, "For so long I made you bear unendurable torments of love."

To which it replied, "By God, nothing ever made me so sick as being cured!"

The Secret

For so long did I hear stories about the angel that assumed concrete form in a woman, and so much did I search for it in the squares, the roads, and alleyways, telling myself that seeing it would be like seeing the Light on the Night of Power.* On the blessed night of the Feast I heard a whispering saying that it would pass by the public fountain when the moon was at its most luminous. So I roamed around the fountain with the determination of a lover and the resolve of a warrior. Then a woman came into sight for a short time. Her unveiled, angelic face took me by storm, and I was overwhelmed by feelings of burning love and rapture. But I did not pursue her, knowing the impossibility of crossing over from the world of mankind to the world of the angels.

At that, the secret of my first love was revealed to me.

The Essence of History

The first time I loved was when I was a child.

I amused myself with my time until death appeared on the horizon.

At the outset of youth I came to know the undying love that is created by the transient lover. I was immersed in the

---

* See note on page 37.

ocean of life; the lover departed, and the memories burned under the noonday sun. A guide deep within me directed me to the golden path that is paved with effort and which leads to unspecified goals.

Sometimes the perfect gentleman makes his appearance, at others the departing lover comes into view.

It became apparent to me that between me and death there was censure, but that I was condemned to hope.

The Man of Destinies

I have not forgotten that man. He was my teacher for a long period of my life. He was well known during his lifetime for having endured a succession of afflictions, an unhappy marriage, and straitened circumstances. But he was also famed for his patience and his ability to live with pain and to steep himself in grief.

When he became advanced in years, a hardening of his arteries was added to his troubles, while his memory began to fail. Among the things he forgot were his losses and all the misery of life he had known. And so, unbeknown to him, his burden was lightened. His illness grew worse and he forgot his wife completely; he refused to have anything to do with her, and began asking himself what she was doing in his house.

Thus much of his distress left him. His illness went to extremes and he forgot his own person and no longer knew who he was, thus scaling the very peak of serenity. In this way he made his escape from the cruel grip of life, so that those who had pitied him counted him fortunate.

Forgiveness

My admiration for you, lady, is beyond reckoning. You illuminate the place with the serenity of your old age. You meet affront with silence and you forgive those who do you harm. I have not known a mother before you with such a sense of loyalty.

One day I said to her, "You are the victim of cruelty and selfishness."

She said with a smile, "Rather am I the victim of love."

And when she saw the astonishment on my face, she said, "You imagine that their behavior toward me emanated from cruelty and selfishness. The truth is that it came from their strong love for their children. It was thus that I used to love them, and because of that my heart has pardoned them."

Laughter

I stood above the opening to the grave, casting a farewell glance at the body of the loved one that they were preparing for its final rest. His ringing laughter came to me from the beautiful past, so I gazed around me but saw only the solemn faces of the mourners.

On the way back by the cemetery road, a friend whispered in my ear, "What about a moment's rest at the café?"

The invitation brought a tremor of delight to my nerves. I took off briskly to where there was someplace to sit, to the glass of ice water, the spicy coffee, and the intimate talk of those who are going to follow those who have gone before.

The Choice

I went to the market carrying something light in weight but of great price. I took my place and awaited my daily bread. The clamor suddenly abated and necks were stretched toward the center. I looked and saw Sitt al-Husn, the fairy-tale princess, walking with swinging stride, advancing with the gait of a veritable queen. She stole both mind and willpower before she had completed a step. I rose to my feet to follow her, leaving behind me my mind, my will, and my means of livelihood.

She entered a small, elegant house, where one encountered a rose garden. A finely attired doorman of awe-inspiring form blocked my way, glaring at me with a disapproving look.

"I am quite prepared to give her all I possess," I said.

To which the man answered in an unequivocal tone, "She does not welcome those who come to her abandoning their work in the market."

The Question

The caravan went plunging into the desert. Leading it was someone playing on a flute to the beating of drums, while the silence around it was like an ocean, and it seemed that there was no end to anything. It occurred to me to inquire where in the caravan its owner wished to walk. A neighbor heard me and said, "In the forefront of the caravan, as befits his status. But what made you ask the question?"

At which another neighbor said, "Rather would he perhaps be at the rear, so that he can observe every movement. What concern is it of yours?"

I found no answer. I thought that the matter was at an end and that I would know the answer when the journey was over. But I found heads drawing together and eyes stealing glances at me, and suspicion spreading among them all. O Lord, how to persuade them that I meant no harm and that I had no less loyalty to the man than any one of them?

A man with a stern face approached me and said, "Leave the caravan and let us be in peace."

I saw no alternative but to depart, and found myself in an absolutely empty space and in permanent distress.

In the Darkness

I was returning home, plunging through the darkness of night, without a ray of light shining out in the blackness. Bumping into a spectral figure, I came to a stop, warily alert as I inquired, "Who are you, O servant of God?"

"Perhaps you are the man of luck I am looking for," he said.

"What luck do you mean?"

"I am inviting you," he said to me pleasantly, "to an evening at my house at which love and entertainment will be on hand."

It occurred to me that he was talking nonsense.

At the moment of doubt, his wavering breathing ceased and I knew that he had vanished. I was tormented by regret

that the opportunity had slipped by me, for it could have
been the hoped-for luck. I continued to roam around in the
darkness, calling out until my voice grew hoarse.

Stronger than Forgetfulness

His face looked straight at me from close by and with
penetrating force, and he whispered in my ear, "Remember me so that you may know me when I meet you."

When I came to, his image had not slipped from
my mind. How greatly was I distracted from him by work
for a time and by fun for a time, and yet he returns with
all his force as though he had not been absent for a single
moment.

Under the pressure of anxiety, I ask myself: When will he
meet me? How does the meeting take place? And what is the
reason for all this?

It is seldom that I drive out apprehensions, even in
warm embraces.

The Intelligence of the Body

They stood on a flat roof carrying on a whispered conversation. He was the taller, she the more handsome.
As for me, I would play with my hoop for a while, then

watch the two of them without understanding. They would disappear for a while into the room on the roof, then return, and I would again steal a look at them with increased confusion.

Understanding came stumbling from across the fiery years.

Sunrise and Sunset

I saw him in two different states.

Once, with the sun rising on him, he looked utterly splendid and sublime. He would talk, and the listener would find wisdom in the words he understood and poetry in what he did not.

Another time, with the sun setting on him, he appeared miserable and puny as he hurried about in rags. He would talk, and the listener would find banality in the words he understood and stupidity in what he did not.

The Look-alike

The extraordinary resemblance between the judge and the accused drew the attention of both the women and the men who accompanied their neighbor, the mother of the accused, to the court.

Some people from among them remembered the

woman's youngest child, whom she had lost in the crowd at the religious festival. But no one identified the judge as the missing boy.

A woman said in a whisper, "The judge is of good family, but as for the missing boy he'd only have fallen into the hands of scoundrels."

The mother had completely forgotten her youngest one and was no longer thinking about anything except her son who was crouching in the dock.

This was until the judge pronounced the awesome sentence.

Then screams resounded through the courtroom.

The Housewife

O housewife, wake up, say your prayers, then spread out your hands in supplication. Get the breakfast ready and call your husband and children to the table.

Help the young ones to wash and frown at those who are too lazy to get up.

Sweep your house and put it in order and amuse yourself by singing a song.

If fate permits, good luck will bring them together around the dinner table.

The children stay on to do their homework and the man goes off to the café for his evening chat.

Wash and comb your hair, change your clothes, and perfume the bedroom with incense.

Today has witnessed something that deserves thanks and praise to God.

Remember that, when the day comes on which all are scattered, each to his own home, and the day on which these memories find no one to remember them.

My Lady the Truth

I knew the degrees of truth in the age of creation.

When the woman squats in front of the basin to do the washing, I squat down in front of her. My hand plays about in the water and my eyes steal a glance at her. When I dissport on the flat roof on nights of full moon, I stretch out my hand into space to grasp the face of the moon.

When she visits the grave on feast days, I concentrate my eyes on its wall so as to see.

How excellent are the enamored companion and the degrees of truth.

Our Laughter
Turned Against Us

The session of evening conversation saw us in the garden at our most complete, in terms of both number and merriment. Conversation took us from one topic to another, like bees among flowers, and the cool air was radiant with our laughter. Time had forgotten us and we it. Then suddenly one of us said, without apparent relevancy, "Just imagine where and how we'll be in half a century!"

The answer, my friend, is exceedingly simple, though at the same time exceedingly complicated, but why are you reminding us of that?

Today only a quarter of a century has passed since that evening. Even so, only two of the companions of that night remain. One of them reminds the other about the words of a dear one who has passed on. They both sigh and imagine as best they can where and how.

Did all those people really live and exchange affection and hope?

The Fact of the Matter

She walked in the shadow of her mother, while he was playing in the street. The thing that made her most happy was her pigtail that exuded the aroma of carnations. As for him, he was playing hopscotch. He stood for a while until the mother passed by with her small daughter. She gave him an equivocal look and he was filled with a feeling of conceit and went running off so that everyone might witness his speed and strength. The mother said a prayer for the good of every creature, whispering, "I fear for her, the way she looks at people; and I fear for him, running about, so take care of them both, O Lord."

There happened to be a man sitting in a corner, one of those who read people's thoughts. He said, as though not to her in particular, "Let her look at him so long as she likes to do so, and as for him, let him run about until his powers dwindle and he calms down."

The Abode of Grace

How beautiful is the bird in its flight and its singing. Once, in a state of intoxicated elation, I called out, "Oh, would that I had been created a bird!" And, all of a sudden, I was changed into a bird that soared into the air and sang and jumped from branch to branch. From my past experience I was on my guard against cats and reptiles, and I adored the rays of the sun.

From days of old I had envied birds their soaring into the air and their seeing the beauty of my beloved, which is not attained by those who wander upon the earth. I became convinced, through futile effort, that there was no way of being successful except through flying and looking down from above the tops of the trees.

I began snatching glances aflame with longing as she strolled in the depths of the house, and I quenched my thirst with the nectar of bliss until I became drunk. One day I saw above the wall of the roof a dish filled with safflower seeds. My mouth watered and I forgot to be on my guard as I flew toward the dish. I alighted on it and began with greedy delight to gobble up the seeds with my beak. Then a hand gently grasped hold of me, and a sweet voice said, "At last you have fallen."

She consigned me to the cage, and her touch sent

through my being a sense of intoxication that comes only from the wine of Paradise.

And whenever the cup of my share of happiness flowed over, she came with her glittering beauty to gaze at me and to give me food and water.

And here I am, steeped in the madness of joyous happiness. In leisure times I look out at the groups of birds on the tree, happy in their flight and their singing. But their singing and their flying is as nothing compared to being close to the beloved.

Abd-Rabbih al-Ta'ih

Sheikh Abd-Rabbih al-Ta'ih first made his appearance in our quarter when he was heard to call out, "A stray one has been born, good fellows."

And when he was asked about the features of the lost boy, he said, "I lost him more than seventy years ago and all his features have slipped my mind."

He was known as Abd-Rabbih al-Ta'ih, the stray one. We would meet him in the street or at the café or in the cave. In the desert cave we would gather with friends, where the joy of communing together would throw them into ecstatic trances. Rightly were they described as the drunks, and their cave as the tavern.

Since I came to know him I have done my best to meet up with him as much as my free time would allow. In his company there is delight and in his talk enjoyment, even though it is sometimes hard for the brain to digest.

Becoming Acquainted

I had a calligrapher friend who was one of the sheikh's disciples, so I asked him to present me to him. On our way to the cave we traversed the desert of the Mamluks. There I saw him in the midst of his companions, exchanging all sorts of intimate conversation in a calm, unsullied atmosphere of elation. My friend presented me to him, but he went on with what he was doing and paid no attention to me, which kindled a sense of embarrassment inside me. However, my friend took me by the hand and we sat at the end of the row. I whispered in his ear, "We'd better go."

He whispered in my ear, "He has accepted your friendship. Had he refused you, he would have done so with a gesture."

So I ended the night with a long, beautiful session of singing. On our return my friend asked me, "What do you think of the place and its people?"

I said, "They have entered my heart without an intermediary. The tie that binds them is enchanting, the place charmingly tranquil and its aroma fragrant."

When Eyes Met

Some time passed before he turned to me and our eyes met. When a smile lit up his features and he had settled beside me, I said, "Accept me into your brotherhood."

"What propels you toward us?" he asked me.

Without hesitation, I said, "I have all but wearied of the world and wish to flee from it."

He said distinctly, "Love of the world is the core of our brotherhood and our enemy is flight."

I felt that I was being freed from the station of perplexity.

Waiting

Yet why this particular cave?

It was said that the lady of the place used to roam about at the spot around the cave at festival times. Many had become possessed by the magic of her beauty and had exerted every effort in searching for her, but without avail. It was said that one day she might choose her partner in the cave. Countless people made their way to the cave, but it was Abd-Rabbih al-Ta'ih and his disciples who had held out until the end.

Most of their conversation and songs were about the beautiful woman.

They wait for acceptance and do not know despair.

An Official

A person whose energy in serving the brethren was incomparable attracted my attention. I asked about him, and Abd-Rabbih al-Ta'ih said:

There is a story about him, so listen to it. Suddenly one night he rushed upon us in our seclusion, saying, "An order has been issued to close down the taverns."

"Our drink is intimate discourse, so drink this glass," I said to him.

I handed him a drink. The magic of the place had pervaded his body and soul, so he drank. Then he left us and went off. On the following night he returned, dressed in ordinary clothes. He said resignedly, "I have left the service and I have come to you."

So we rejoiced and glorified God, and from that moment he was merged in our affection. At feast times he would sing and dance until daybreak.

A Malady

Sheikh Abd-Rabbih al-Ta'ih said:

"Yesterday as I was returning just before dawn from the evening gathering, my way was blocked in the darkness of the lane by a person whose features I could not make out. He said to me, 'I come to you from beyond the stars.'

"I was moved by pride and I said joyfully, 'Is it for my sake that you have descended?'

"In a tone of voice that was not devoid of displeasure, he said, 'You are not yet free of conceit!'

"And he disappeared upward with the speed of lightning. I would that he would return and forgive me."

So I asked him, "What were you proposing to demand of him?"

He answered, ignoring my question, "Life is a flood of memories that pours forth into the sea of forgetfulness. As for death, it is the deeply rooted truth."

The Complaint

The cave was peopled with bosom friends, elation melting the very stones.

Somebody blew out the candles and the noise of breathing could be heard in the pitch-black darkness. A voice reached out to them saying, "In heaven they have become displeased with despicable actions and disagreeable smells."

The voice departed, leaving a heavy silence behind, so one of them said, "It's a message."

Said another, "Rather is it an order."

They rushed off to the markets, attacking everything despicable and disagreeable.

The gentlemen were angry; they raged with anger and brandished sticks.

Dancing in the Air

Once the sheikh said to me that the stories that are published are not true stories. Wanting to present me with a truthful story, he said:

On a spring morning an uproar drew me toward the green doorway to a saint's tomb. I waded through a barrier of human beings who were gathered around a man and a woman who were said to be from among the possessed who congregate at al-Husayn Mosque. Then passionate love enticed them, so they renounced the world of secrets for the world of love. We saw them staggering from the effects of intoxication and chanting erotic songs.

People would have assaulted them had it not been for the intervention of the police.

With time the matter was forgotten. One morning, while walking in the desert, I saw a cloud descending like an airplane or a ship until it came clearly within sight.

I saw on its surface a man and a woman dancing, and I heard their voices saying, "When will you rise up, Abd-Rabbih?"

A Fragrance from Afar

Sheikh Abd-Rabbih al-Ta'ih said:
My feet carried me to the deserted tomb from which all those who used to concern themselves with remembering him had departed. I found it on the point of collapsing and with the appearance of imminent obliteration. A faint call issued from my memory as a group of men and women advanced toward me, as they had once been wont to do. One of them repeated to me several times, "Nothing passes my lips before I hear the morning song on the radio."

Eternity

Sheikh Abd-Rabbih al-Ta'ih said:

I stood before the holy tomb as I asked God for health and long life. An old beggar with tattered clothes approached me. "Do you really want long life?" he asked me.

"Who does not wish it?" I said, with the terseness of someone not wanting to talk to him.

He presented me with a small, closed receptacle and said, "Here you have the flavor of eternity—whoever tastes of it will not endure death."

I smiled disdainfully, and he said, "I have dealt with it for thousands of years and I am still weighed down by the burdens of life, generation after generation."

I mumbled in derision, "What a happy man you are!"

"Those," he said despondently, "are the words of someone who has not suffered the passing of the ages, the succession of circumstances, the growing of knowledge, the demise of loved ones, and the burying of grandchildren."

Adjusting to his strange appearance, I inquired, "Who could you be among the men of the age?"

He answered sadly, "I was the master of existence—have you not seen my great statue? With the setting of each sun I lament my wasted days, my declining countries, and my transitory gods."

To Hear Is to Obey

Sheikh Abd-Rabbih al-Ta'ih said:

I told him humbly, my eyes not leaving his countenance, "I have never seen anyone so splendid."

"It is thanks to God, Lord of the Worlds," he said, smiling.

"I would like to know who you are, sir."

"I am he who used to wake you from sleep before sunrise," he said quietly, as though remembering. "I am he who helped you against laziness, so that you began to work."

I thought deeply about what he had said, and he continued. "It was I who spurred you on to the love of knowledge."

"Yes, yes!" I exclaimed.

"And the beauty of existence, it was I who guided you to its fountainheads."

"I am forever indebted to you."

A tense silence reigned. Feeling that he had come to demand something of me, I said, "I am at your disposal."

He said with intense calmness, "I went away so as to put the finishing touch to my work."

A Question About the World

I asked Sheikh Abd-Rabbih about what was said of his love of women, food, poetry, knowledge, and singing, and he answered earnestly, "That is thanks to the King, the Grantor."

I called his attention to the censuring of the world by the saints, to which he said, "They are censuring the corruption that took possession of it."

Walking in the Dark

Sheikh Abd-Rabbih al-Ta'ih said:

I knew the man during two phases of his long life.

I knew him in his youth, when he loved worship and would constantly be around the mosque, spellbound from listening to the holy Qur'an. And in his old age, when his destiny led him to the tavern and he had become addicted to wine, oblivious of what did not concern him. He would return home in the final part of the night, reeling drunkenly and singing the songs of youth as he plunged through the pitch-black darkness.

Those who loved him warned him about walking in the dark, to which he said, "Guardian angels surround me and from my head shines a light that illuminates the place."

A Saying

Sheikh Abd-Rabbih said one night at the evening gathering of the cave:

How beautiful are the stories of love—may God forgive the time that gives them life and causes their death.

Definition

I asked Sheikh Abd-Rabbih, "What is the sign of unbelief?"

He replied without hesitation, "Discontent."

My Beautiful Lady

Said Sheikh Abd-Rabbih:

This happened when I was moving between childhood and boyhood.

I saw a woman seated on the middle sofa, under the invocation "In the Name of God, the Merciful, the Compassionate." In my life I had seen nothing more beautiful. She smiled at me, so I went up to her, at which she leaned over me, kissed me, and gave me a piece of that sweet called *malban*. I kept the secret so that the giving might continue. Whenever I went to the room I would return spoiled, with a kiss and a piece of *malban*.

Then, one day, I went as usual and found the room empty.

Would I lose both beauty and happiness?

I asked my mother about the beautiful and generous guest.

She was amazed at my question, as was my father, and I began swearing by the most sacred oaths that it had been so.

They did not believe a word of what I had recounted, and for a long time they were assailed by anxiety for me.

A feeling of dejection remained hidden deep within me until the nights of the new moon appeared.

On the Point of Escape

Sheikh Abd-Rabbih al-Ta'ih spoke and said:
Once I was impelled by ecstasy of rapture to persist in rapture until I aspired to leap from the lesser rapture to the greater rapture, so I asked of God to grant me a happy conclusion.

At that a voice whispered in my ear, "God does not bless those who flee."

When

I asked Sheikh Abd-Rabbih al-Ta'ih:
"When will the state of the country be sound?"
He replied, "When its people believe that the end result

of cowardice is more disastrous than that of behaving with integrity."

The Postman

O n one of the nights of the cave there was a strong wind and a heavy downpour of rain. Gusts of air penetrating through from the entrance played with the wispy flames of the candles, and hearts beat violently. Eyes were directed at the entrance and they waited, hearts beating even more wildly.

One of them whispered, "They say that the night of this year is blessed."

Hearts were drawn toward the entrance with all the strength they possessed.

A whistling came to them from afar and they jumped to their feet. At that moment the postman entered in his familiar uniform and with his bag almost drenched from the water soaking his clothes.

Calmly he gave to each outstretched hand a letter, then left without uttering a word.

They broke open the envelopes and looked at the letters by the light of the candles. They found that they were blank pieces of paper with nothing on them.

Abd-Rabbih exclaimed, "The outcome will be known to those that are patient."

Azrael

Sheikh Abd-Rabbih al-Ta'ih said:

The official summoned me one day and said, "Your words impel people to insurrection, so watch out!"

I said to him, "I feel sorry for someone whose duty demands that he defend robbers and give chase to honest folk!"

"This is a final warning," he shouted at me.

As Azrael used to hasten to my assistance at times of misfortune, he was visible to the official for several seconds, so that his limbs trembled and he fell from his chair, exclaiming, "May God be between me and you!"

The Choice

Sheikh Abd-Rabbih al-Ta'ih said:

A beautiful woman came to me asking my opinion in a matter that concerned her. In providing her with the answer, I read her star of destiny on her radiant forehead and said, "In front of you are two paths: the path of virtue and heaven and the path of love and bearing children."

She said with a modest smile, "The Possessor of Glory has prepared me for love and the bearing of children, and I shall not oppose His wish."

Mercy

I asked Sheikh Abd-Rabbih al-Ta'ih, "How can such events occur in a world made by a Merciful, Compassionate One?"

He answered calmly, "Were He not Merciful and Compassionate they would not occur."

The Woman Preacher

Sheikh Abd-Rabbih al-Ta'ih said:
I was stopped in the market by a woman who was a prodigy of beauty, and she asked me, "Shall I counsel you, O preacher?"

"Welcome to what you may have to say," I said confidently.

She said, "Do not turn away from me, lest you regret for your lifetime the loss of the greatest boon."

The Sheepfold

Sheikh Abd-Rabbih al-Ta'ih said:
I dreamed that I was standing in a vast sheepfold. The sheep were eating and drinking and making love in peace and tranquillity. I wished that I were one of them—a ram of great strength and beauty. Then one day the owner

of the sheepfold came, followed by the butcher carrying his knife.

The End of the Ordeal

I asked Sheikh Abd-Rabbih al-Ta'ih:
"How will the ordeal we are suffering end?"
He answered, "If we come out safe, that's a mercy; and if we come out doomed, that is justice."

Unbelievable

Sheikh Abd-Rabbih al-Ta'ih said:
A man came to me and said, "Don't believe it—you are merely the son of blind chance, the struggle of ethnic elements. Without a purpose you came, without a purpose you will go, and it will be as if you had not been."
I said to him, "It previously happened that your father believed what must not be believed, and he forfeited ease of mind and felicity."

The Beautiful Act

Sheikh Abd-Rabbih al-Ta'ih spoke and said:

One day I came across a suitcase containing a treasure of money. It also had in it indications as to its owner and his address. As he was one of those corrupt people with which the country has been afflicted, I decided not to return it to him. I put it secretly in the basement of a poor man who was one of our friends and was known for his piety. I had no doubt that he would spend it in the cause of God. Then I learned that he had returned it to its owner, waiving his legal right to it, and I was saddened and sorry. Then our poor pious friend died, so I hastened to him, washed him, enshrouded him, carried him to the mosque, and said the prayers over him. When the prayers were finished, I noticed among the worshipers behind the bier the corrupt rich man, weeping bitterly.

My heart was deeply touched and I said, "Glory be to You, O Possessor of Sovereignty. You know what we do not know—perhaps the awakening came from no one knows where by Your permission."

A Supplication

I was afflicted by an indisposition, and Sheikh Abd-Rabbih al-Ta'ih visited me. He made an incantation over me, and said a prayer for me with the words "O God, bestow upon him a good conclusion, which is love."

The Bridegroom

I asked Sheikh Abd-Rabbih al-Ta'ih about his ideal among those people with whom he had been closely associated, and he said:

A good man whose miracles were manifested by his perseverance in the service of people and the remembrance of God; on his hundredth birthday he drank, danced, sang, and married a virgin of twenty.

And on the wedding night there came a troop of angels, who perfumed him with incense from the mountains of Qaf at the end of the earth.

Isolation

Sheikh Abd-Rabbih al-Ta'ih said:

I was crossing a square crammed with people when I saw a man who was possessed, beating about him with his stick in all directions, as though fighting against unseen creatures, until his powers failed him and his strength gave out. Then he seated himself on the pavement and set about drying his sweat. All the while no one paid any attention to him, so I approached and asked him, "What were you doing, O servant of God?"

He answered furiously, "I was fighting a power that had come to annihilate the people, but no one understood what I was doing, and no one assisted me."

The Voice of the Tomb

Sheikh Abd-Rabbih al-Ta'ih said:

I was walking along the road to the cemeteries as I returned from the evening's entertainment at the tavern. A voice from a tomb reached me, asking, "Why have you stopped visiting us and talking with us?"

I answered, "You enjoy talking about nothing except death and the dead, and I have tired of it."

The Surface of the Heart

Sheikh Abd-Rabbih al-Ta'ih said:

I kept looking at my heart in the mirror of my goblet, and I was appalled by its venial sins. I said to it, "Who would believe that you had experienced all that love? How is it you were a world teeming with women, men, and things?"

There was no evidence, O heart of mine, of the truth of what was, except for tears that gushed forth into the air and disappeared in space.

Constancy

I saw Sheikh Abd-Rabbih al-Ta'ih walking in a funeral procession.

Knowing as I did that he only joined such processions

when they were for good people, I joined his row and continued on until we had said the prayers over the dead man together. Then I asked the sheikh about him, and he said, "A noble man, and how rare are noble men. Despite his advanced years he refused to renounce love until he perished."

That Love

I said to Sheikh Abd-Rabbih al-Ta'ih, "I heard some people holding against you your intense love for the world."

He said, "Love of the world is one of the signs of gratitude, and evidence of a craving for everything beautiful, and one of the distinguishing marks of patience."

The Slumber of Death

Sheikh Abd-Rabbih al-Ta'ih said, "Once I was more than usually disturbed by the idea of death. I was about to go to sleep when it occurred to me that death might visit me while I slept and that the morning would not shine on me. I asked God for well-being out of pity for people who were awaiting my help the following day."

He prayed to God for a long time for His forgiveness, then murmured, "How often have I imbibed the depth of the glorification of God in the station of confusion."

The Flood

Sheikh Abd-Rabbih al-Ta'ih said:

The Flood will come tomorrow or after tomorrow. It will sweep away corruption and the feebly corrupt, and no one will remain except for a minority of the efficient. A new city will be set up, from the heart of which will arise a new life. Would that your life should go on long enough, Abd-Rabbih, for you to live for even one day in the city that is to come.

On Trade

Sheikh Abd-Rabbih al-Ta'ih said:

Beware, for I have found no trade more profitable than the selling of dreams.

The Sweet Time

Sheikh Abd-Rabbih al-Ta'ih said:

I found myself on a hill looking at a cinema screen stretched out in space. A corps of beautiful girls danced and sang to a cosmic rhythm, by their movements scattering pearls of resplendent light.

I asked in a loud voice, "Who are you?"

To which they answered, "We are the few sweet days that

have passed in utter splendor and serenity, untarnished by vexation."

The Two Dancers

S heikh Abd-Rabbih al-Ta'ih said:
    Nothing alarmed me as did the sight of life dancing with death to that rhythm we hear only once in a whole lifetime.

The Pursuer

S heikh Abd-Rabbih al-Ta'ih said:
    It pursues me from the cradle to the grave: love.

ᕦ   ᕦ   ᕦ

Sheikh Abd-Rabbih al-Ta'ih said:
    It became generally known in the quarter that the beautiful woman would give herself to the winner. The young men dedicated themselves wholeheartedly to the contest. The winner went off to the woman intoxicated with happiness, staggering with exhaustion. At her feet he threw himself down, wedded to passion, a prey to fatigue. He went on gazing happily at her until overcome by drowsiness.

ᕦ   ᕦ   ᕦ

Sheikh Abd-Rabbih al-Ta'ih said:

The reception room has seen even me, as I waited, hoping for success.

The father enters, dignified and lovable, but cautioning against fetters and consequences.

An inner voice called to me to make my escape.

Then she comes, tripping along bashfully, and I fall into the abyss.

Bashfulness

Sheikh Abd-Rabbih al-Ta'ih said:
Nothing revealed itself to my eyes except the flush of her cheeks, the sweetness of her bashfulness.

I repeat the question and she plunges more deeply into silence.

She bestows liberally everything of value, but from speech she shies away.

The Guest

Sheikh Abd-Rabbih al-Ta'ih said:
Our house was crowded with loved ones.

One day, a guest whom I had not previously seen came to stay.

Desiring to make him feel comfortable, my father sent me far off to play.

When I returned, I found the house empty, with no trace of the guest or of the loved ones.

The Sadness of Life

Sheikh Abd-Rabbih al-Ta'ih was asked whether life feels sad about anyone.

He replied, "Yes, if he is one of its faithful lovers."

Perfection

Sheikh Abd-Rabbih al-Ta'ih said:

Perfection is a dream that lives in the imagination. If it were to be realized in existence, life for any living creature would not be pleasant.

Magic

Sheikh Abd-Rabbih al-Ta'ih said:

Life appears to be a chain of struggles, tears, and fears, and yet it has a magic that enchants and intoxicates.

Faithfulness in Comely Women

Sheikh Abd-Rabbih al-Ta'ih said:
    Oh, that beautiful woman who knows no faithfulness!
    Neither is she satisfied, nor do her lovers learn a lesson.

Our Nature

Once I said to Sheikh Abd-Rabbih al-Ta'ih, "I might welcome general exhaustion, but a single month's holiday makes me depressed."
    He said, "Our nature is to love life and to hate death."

The Truthful Lie

Sheikh Abd-Rabbih al-Ta'ih said:
    Some of the lies of life spurt forth in truth.

Volition

Sheikh Abd-Rabbih al-Ta'ih said:
    In the universe floats the will, and in the will floats the universe.

Mutual Love

Sheikh Abd-Rabbih al-Ta'ih said:
They are two. By its strength the first created the other, and by its weakness the other created the first.

Comprehension

Sheikh Abd-Rabbih al-Ta'ih said:
He opened the gate of infinity when He said, "Do you not comprehend?"

A Telegram

Sheikh Abd-Rabbih al-Ta'ih said:
On one of the unforgettable nights of the cave I was overcome by intoxication after insomnia and confusion. At which an atom floating in the depths of the universe whispered in my psyche that I should set my mind at rest.

A Meeting in the Dark

Sheikh Abd-Rabbih al-Ta'ih said:

In early youth I had this dream:

I saw the desert stretching away in front of me, so I ventured into it, drunk with my freedom. When evening came upon me I wanted to return, but I missed my way and was as lost in the darkness as a wandering breeze. I was seized by fear and despair. I looked at the sky but the stars told me nothing. I was aware of people continually brushing against my face, and I inquired, "Who's there?"

A quiet voice answered me, "Follow my form."

So I followed it, yielding myself up to the fates. As time went by and nothing untoward happened, I was reassured. The form thrust a long-necked bottle into my hand and asked me to drink. I took a thirst-quenching drink and the effect coursed through me from head to foot.

"What drink is this?" I asked.

"Wine that I made in my house," answered the form.

I would have become alarmed were it not that elation caused me to rise above my apprehensions.

The harbingers of sunrise showed as we were walking.

I caught a glimpse of the form's face in the light of the first rays, and I found that it was the face of a woman, the likes of whose beauty I had never seen.

I begged her to stop for a while. I knelt in front of her humbly and embraced her in my arms.

Inhalation/Exhalation

Sheikh Abd-Rabbih al-Ta'ih said:
    With the inhalation of the universe and its exhalation, all joys and pains are in raptures.

Freedom

Sheikh Abd-Rabbih al-Ta'ih said:
    The nearest man comes to his Lord is when he is exercising his freedom correctly.

The Secret

Sheikh Abd-Rabbih al-Ta'ih used not to conceal his passion for women. He said, "Love is the key to the secrets of existence."

The Talk of Death

Sheikh Abd-Rabbih al-Ta'ih said:
    I saw death in the guise of a man far advanced in years. It said reprovingly, "If I abstained from my work for a whole year, I would force you to affirm my usefulness."

Optimism

I asked Sheikh Abd-Rabbih al-Ta'ih, "Why does optimism prevail with you?"

He answered, "Because we still admire beautiful words even though we do not practice them."

What You Wish

In immersing himself in the life of this world, Sheikh Abd-Rabbih al-Ta'ih aroused the astonishment of some of the disciples, so he said to them, "Do what you wish provided you do not forget your basic function, which is to leave something behind you."

Comedy and Tragedy

Sheikh Abd-Rabbih al-Ta'ih said:

He who has lost his faith has lost life and death.

Speed

Sheikh Abd-Rabbih al-Ta'ih said:

We are hardly done with getting the house in order when there comes to us the call to depart.

The Consultant

Sheikh Abd-Rabbih al-Ta'ih said:

In my desire for guidance I decided to visit your friend whose iniquity and corruption have made the very earth cry out. I asked to meet him and was met by his consultant, who gave me coffee. Our eyes met for an instant and I knew him to be a devil in disguise. When he sensed that I knew him for what he was, he laughed and said, "I've lost this round, so I'll play another."

The Powerful Adversary

Sheikh Abd-Rabbih al-Ta'ih said:

O you who have awakened the heart in the temporal world, I bear witness that you have created the powerful adversary who defies death.

A Sea

Sheikh Abd-Rabbih al-Ta'ih said:
   I found myself in a sea in which the waves of joy and sorrow were clashing against each other.

Thanks

Sheikh Abd-Rabbih al-Ta'ih said:
   Praise be to God, Whose existence has saved us from frivolous play in the world and from perdition in the After-life.

A Heartbeat

Sheikh Abd-Rabbih al-Ta'ih said:
   A single beat from the heart of a lover is capable of driving out a hundred sorrows.

I Am Love

Sheikh Abd-Rabbih al-Ta'ih said:
  We were in the cave conversing intimately when a voice rang out, saying, "I am love. Were it not for me the water would dry up, the air would become putrid, and death would strut about in every corner."

Invasion

Sheikh Abd-Rabbih al-Ta'ih said:
  One day I tried to be detached, but the sighings of mankind invaded my seclusion.

Love and the Beloved

Sheikh Abd-Rabbih al-Ta'ih said:
  The beloved may absent herself from existence, but love does not.

Do Not Curse

Sheikh Abd-Rabbih al-Ta'ih said:

Do not curse the world, for it hardly has a hand in what occurs in it.

Offering Condolences

Sheikh Abd-Rabbih al-Ta'ih said:

A man came to me complaining and I asked him what was wrong. He said, "I am drowning in the sea of pleasures, and yet I am not satisfied."

I said to him, "I shall visit you on the day when you are satisfied, so that I may offer you my condolences."

The World and the Afterlife

Sheikh Abd-Rabbih al-Ta'ih said:

If you have sincerely loved the world, the Afterlife will love you warmly.

Without Welcome

Sheikh Abd-Rabbih al-Ta'ih said:
   The friend to whom we seldom extend a welcome is death.

The Secret

Sheikh Abd-Rabbih al-Ta'ih said:
   As you love, so will you be.

The Middle Way

Sheikh Abd-Rabbih al-Ta'ih said:
   Some people are preoccupied with life and others are preoccupied with death. As for me, my position is firmly fixed in the middle way.

Staggering

Sheikh Abd-Rabbih al-Ta'ih said:
   It has been decreed that man shall walk staggering between pleasure and pain.

The Two Jewels

Sheikh Abd-Rabbih al-Ta'ih said:
Two jewels are charged with looking after the golden door, saying to the one who knocks, "Come forward, for there is no escape." They are love and death.

The Daily Round

Sheikh Abd-Rabbih al-Ta'ih said:
I stretched myself out on the green earth under the light of the moon, roaming in a vision. The earth whispered complainingly in my ear, "They are competing for my daily bread, and all I have done is to reclaim what had previously been bestowed on me."

The Secret Behind the Secret

Sheikh Abd-Rabbih al-Ta'ih said:
I said to life, "You are truly one of the secrets of the Giver." And life said shyly, "My children ask me and find I have only the question."

The Final Time

I asked Sheikh Abd-Rabbih al-Ta'ih, "How should we behave with the time of contentment and joy?"

He answered, "Regard it as being the final time that remains to you."

Look

Sheikh Abd-Rabbih al-Ta'ih said:

If you are afflicted with doubt, then look at length in the mirror of your self.

The Breeze of Love

Sheikh Abd-Rabbih al-Ta'ih said:

The breeze of love blows for an hour and makes amends for the ill winds of the whole of a lifetime.

The Sermon of the Dawn

Sheikh Abd-Rabbih al-Ta'ih said to the evening companions of the cave:

Do not complain of the world. Do not search for wisdom behind those of its acts that are baffling. Save your strength for what is beneficial, and be content with what has been decreed. And if you are lured by an inclination toward melancholy, then treat it with love and song.

Time

Sheikh Abd-Rabbih al-Ta'ih said:

Time is entitled to imagine that it is more powerful than any destructive force, but it realizes its aims soundlessly through love.

The Universal Struggle

Sheikh Abd-Rabbih al-Ta'ih said:

The most universal struggle in existence is the one between love and death.

The Origin

Sheikh Abd-Rabbih al-Ta'ih said:
Evil has encircled man from all sides, so man has devised good in all courses of action.

The Imagination

Sheikh Abd-Rabbih al-Ta'ih said:
The long-lived may one day realize that he is longer-lived than the most beautiful symbols of life.

The Green Bird

Sheikh Abd-Rabbih al-Ta'ih said:
I loved to the full, and I soared on the wings of success, and singing on the nights of the full moon filled me with delight. At sunset the green bird alighted and warbled, saddening me without my comprehending any meaning in it.

The Heartbeat

Sheikh Abd-Rabbih al-Ta'ih said:

There is nothing between the lifting of the veil from the face of the bride and the lowering of it over her corpse but a moment that is like a heartbeat.

Movement

Sheikh Abd-Rabbih al-Ta'ih said:

People came to me and said that they had decided to stand still until they discovered the meaning of life. I said to them, "Move about without delay, for the meaning is concealed in movement."

Do Not Regret

Sheikh Abd-Rabbih al-Ta'ih said:

Beat, O heart of mine, and love everything beautiful, and weep with copious tears; but do not regret.

Good Conclusion

Sheikh Abd-Rabbih al-Ta'ih said:
How beautiful it is to bid someone farewell with each of you holding the other in more esteem.

A Sign

Sheikh Abd-Rabbih al-Ta'ih said:
I propose hanging a sign over the entrance to the cave saying, "May God perpetuate the empire of your beauty."

That Which Fills Space

Sheikh Abd-Rabbih al-Ta'ih said:
Were it not for the whisperings of beautiful secrets floating in space, shooting meteors would mercilessly hurl themselves down upon the earth.

Yearning

Sheikh Abd-Rabbih al-Ta'ih said:
What I endured from desire made my life a yearning concealed in nostalgia.

Foolishness

Sheikh Abd-Rabbih al-Ta'ih said:
There is no one more foolish than the foolish believer, except for the foolish unbeliever.

Singing

Sheikh Abd-Rabbih al-Ta'ih said:
Singing is the dialogue of hearts in love.

Now

Sheikh Abd-Rabbih al-Ta'ih said:
The present is a light that flickers between two darknesses.

The Debt

Sheikh Abd-Rabbih al-Ta'ih said:
   Life is a heavy debt—may God have mercy on him who has paid it off.

Pardon

Sheikh Abd-Rabbih al-Ta'ih said:
   The strongest of all are they who pardon.

A Reminder

Sheikh Abd-Rabbih al-Ta'ih said:
   When death gathers to itself another, it reminds us that we are still delighting in the boon of living.

The Oasis

Sheikh Abd-Rabbih al-Ta'ih said:
   In the desert is an oasis that is the hope of him who has lost his way.

The Garden

Sheikh Abd-Rabbih al-Ta'ih said:

How beautiful is peace of mind in a rose garden.

Release

On the eve of the festival we were brought together in the cave. No one failed to turn up.

Outside, the cold winds howled and raged.

Inside, every breast gave lavishly of its hankering until an elation of song was diffused.

Sheikh Abd-Rabbih al-Ta'ih said, "Happy is he who has fulfilled his task in the market or who has defied grief."

We lowered our eyes shyly and gave ear to the immemorial reed pipe of the shepherd.

The sheikh said, "Look at the door of the cave and don't turn your gaze from it."

Hearts throbbed until their very roots trembled in anticipation of release.

In our anxiety, the inner vision saw it, the inner mind heard it.

About the Author

Naguib Mahfouz was born on December 11, 1911, in the old al-Gamaliyya quarter of Cairo, the youngest of seven children in a family of four other boys and two girls. Although he had many siblings, Mahfouz felt like an only child because the next-youngest brother was ten years older than him. He mourned his lack of normal sibling bonds, which is evidenced by the portrayal of fraternal relationships in much of his work. But his childhood was a happy one—the family was stable and loving, and religion played a very important role in their life—and in his work there are many signs of Mahfouz's affection for his early childhood.

He spent nine or ten years in al-Gamaliyya, which plays an important role in his earlier, realistic novels such as *Midaq Alley* and *The Cairo Trilogy,* and figures symbolically and in terms of characters and physical images in later books like *Children of the Alley* and *The Harafish*. In these works, the alley of his childhood is a kind of microcosm of Egyptian society. The family house also seems to have inspired Mahfouz, and serves as the model for the Abd al-Jawad family house in *The Cairo Trilogy*. Mahfouz recalls in these novels the house's various rooms and secret places, including the roof, which becomes a scene for family gatherings and the meetings of lovers.

His family moved to Abbasiya, a new suburban district, around 1920, which like al-Gamaliyya is frequently evoked in his novels and short stories. This is where, like Kamal in *The Cairo Trilogy*, Mahfouz experienced love for the first time. The 1919 Revolution (an uprising against the British) also had a lasting effect on Mahfouz, leaving him with his first real sense of nationalist feeling and influencing his writings greatly. Interestingly, he became disillusioned with the Revolution of 1952, but took issue with the practices, not the principles. He voiced his criticisms loudly in his writings of the 1960s, but unlike many other intellectuals of the time, he was never arrested by Nasser.

Mahfouz started writing in primary school, when he was a fan of detective, historical, and adventure novels. In secondary school he moved on to the innovators of Arabic fiction—Taha Hussein, Mohammed Hussein Heikal, Ibrahim al-Mazni—who served him as models for the short story.

Despite his penchant for writing, and his early facility with mathematics and the sciences, Mahfouz elected to study philosophy at Fuad I University (now Cairo University) in 1930 and graduated in 1934. His interest in philosophy was partly inspired by the writings of Abbas al-Aqqad. Beginning in secondary school and continuing through his university years, he published more than forty articles in various magazines and newspapers, most of which dealt with philosophical and psychological issues and were heavily influenced by Henri Bergson.

From 1934 until his retirement in 1971 at the age of sixty, he worked in a variety of government departments as a civil servant. He held a secretarial post at Cairo University until 1938, when he moved to the Ministry of Religious Endowments to work as a parliamentary secretary to the minister. In 1945 he requested and received transfer to the al-Ghuri library near his birthplace, al-

Gamaliyya. During his time there he managed the Good Loan Project, an interest-free loan scheme for the poor. It was a very happy time for him, and he had plenty of opportunity to observe the life of the area and to read Western literature, including his favorites: Shakespeare, Conrad, Melville, Flaubert, Stendhal, Tolstoy, Proust, O'Neill, Shaw, Ibsen, and Strindberg.

In the 1950s he worked as the secretary to the Minister of National Guidance, director of the Film Censorship Office, director-general of the Film Support Organization, advisor to the General Organization for Film Industry, and finally as advisor to the Minister of Culture.

His first novel, *The Game of Fates,* was published in 1939, and since then he has written thirty-four more novels and fourteen collections of short stories. From the late 1940s to the early 1980s he worked on some twenty-five screenplays, which seems to have influenced such devices as montage and flashback in his prose writings. Over thirty Egyptian films have been based on Mahfouz's novels and short stories, but strangely, he was never interested in adapting his own books for the screen; the screenplay adaptations were done by others. He was invited to be a writer emeritus at *al-Ahram* newspaper in 1971.

Mahfouz has received the Egyptian State Prize twice for his writings, and numerous other awards, including the Nobel Prize for Literature in 1988. The Swedish Academy of Letters, in awarding Mahfouz the Nobel Prize, noted that Mahfouz, "through works rich in nuance—now clear-sightedly realistic, now evocatively ambiguous—has formed an Arabic narrative art that applies to all mankind."

In 1989 he received the Presidential Medal from the American University in Cairo, which also awarded him an honorary doctorate in June 1995. In 1992 he was elected an honorary member of the American Academy and Institute of Arts and Letters.

On October 14, 1994, he was attacked and stabbed in the neck outside his home. He is still making a slow and painful recovery, and has not yet regained full use of his right arm and hand. Although unable to write physically, he still contributes a weekly column to *al-Ahram* newspaper through conversation with his friend, the writer Mohammed Salmawy.

Mahfouz remained a bachelor until 1954, when he married at

the age of forty-three. He and his wife have two daughters and live in Agouza, a Nileside suburb of Cairo. He has left Egypt only three times in his life, once to Yemen, once to Yugoslavia, and once to England for surgery.

About the Translator

Denys Johnson-Davies has published over twenty volumes of short stories, novels, and poetry translated from modern Arabic literature, most recently Naguib Mahfouz's *Arabian Nights and Days*.